LIFE WITHOUT PAROLE

LIFE WITHOUT PAROLE

Living and Dying in Prison Today

FIFTH EDITION

Victor Hassine
Inmate AM4737

Edited by

Robert Johnson
American University

Sonia Tabriz
The George Washington University Law School

New York Oxford
OXFORD UNIVERSITY PRESS
2011

Oxford University Press, Inc., publishes works that further Oxford University's objective of excellence in research, scholarship, and education.

Oxford New York
Auckland Cape Town Dar es Salaam Hong Kong Karachi
Kuala Lumpur Madrid Melbourne Mexico City Nairobi
New Delhi Shanghai Taipei Toronto

With offices in
Argentina Austria Brazil Chile Czech Republic France Greece
Guatemala Hungary Italy Japan Poland Portugal Singapore
South Korea Switzerland Thailand Turkey Ukraine Vietnam

For titles covered by Section 112 of the US Higher Education Opportunity Act, please visit www.oup.com/us/he for the latest information about pricing and alternate formats.

Published by Oxford University Press, Inc.
198 Madison Avenue, New York, New York 10016
http://www.oup.com

Library of Congress Cataloging-in-Publication Data

Hassine, Victor, 1955–2008
Life without parole : living and dying in prison today / Victor Hassine ; edited by Robert Johnson, Sonia Tabriz.—5th ed.
p. cm.
ISBN 978-0-19-977405-0 (alk. paper)
1. Prisoners—Pennsylvania—Case studies. 2. Hassine, Victor, 1955–
3. Life imprisonment—Pennsylvania—Case studies. 4. Prisons—Pennsylvania—Case studies. 5. Graterford State Correctional Institution. I. Johnson, Robert, 1948–
II. Tabriz, Sonia. III. Title.
HV9475.P2H37 2011
365'.60922748—dc22 2010039423

Printed in the United States of America
on acid-free paper

This book is a tribute to Victor Hassine
Scholar, teacher, colleague
Son, brother, and friend

This book, and indeed all my work, is dedicated to my wife, Deirdra McLaughlin, the person I most admire and whose counsel I seek in all matters;

And to Sonia Tabriz—my young colleague and valued friend, co-editor and co-author of writing projects done and yet to come—for the vision, insight, and care she brought to the task of revising this work, which now stands as a proud monument to Victor Hassine's life.

—Robert Johnson

I wish to dedicate this book to my family—without your unconditional love and unwavering support I would not be the person I am today;

And to my distinguished mentor and friend, Robert Johnson—it has been an honor and will remain a privilege working with and learning from you.

—Sonia Tabriz

CONTENTS

ABOUT THIS BOOK

This edition of Victor Hassine's *Life Without Parole* has a new subtitle and a new format. The original subtitle, *Living in Prison Today,* has been changed to *Living and Dying in Prison Today* to honor Hassine's tragic death by suicide as he approached his fourth decade behind bars. Earlier iterations of this book reflected the unfolding of a life in progress, with all the tentativeness, false starts, and rethinking of one's existence that attend any life, perhaps especially a life confined to prison. Prisons spawn introspection; a life in prison is one that begs for examination, if not explanation. This latest edition is the tale of a life that has come to a close. As a result, Victor Hassine's life is, sadly, one that can be seen whole and told as a flowing story with a beginning, middle, and end, as well as a cautionary message. In this edition, we let Victor Hassine's life speak for itself.

Earlier versions of this book were composed of segregated parts, each consisting of chapters preceded by brief summative editors' introductions. While prior editions met with considerable success over the years, they had accumulated excesses along the way that diluted Hassine's profound message. We cut the extraneous and at times redundant material, integrating the various disconnected sections into a fluid narrative that follows the contours of Victor Hassine's life and death behind bars. For the first time, the reader enters detention with Hassine and joins him on his long journey serving a life-without-parole sentence. We also excised the editors' introductions and replaced them with two essays that now bookend Hassine's text. These essays, co-authored by the editors of this edition, engage the reader in a new way of understanding life and death in prison and offer insights that supplement Hassine's own perceptions. Finally, in striving to capture and convey Hassine's life story, we have included in this edition three of his original and applauded works of fiction. Showcased in the final chapter of this book are short stories that eloquently examine fear, loss, and hope—themes central to the human condition in and out of prison.

The Editors would like to thank those who reviewed the book for their insights: Kelly Asmussen, Peru State College; Ashley G. Blackburn, University of North Texas; Fran Buntman, George Washington University; Jill D'Angelo, Buffalo State College; Charles Hanna, Duquesne University; Jessie L. Krienert, Illinois State University; Robert Swan, University of South Dakota; John Tahiliani, Worcester State College; and Kiesha Warren-Gordon, Ball State University.

ABOUT THE AUTHOR

Victor Hassine was born on June 20, 1955 and immigrated to Trenton, New Jersey after his family was exiled from Egypt for religious reasons. In 1966, Hassine became an American citizen and by 1977 he had graduated from Dickinson College with majors in political science and history. In November of 1980, shortly after graduating from New York Law School, Hassine was arrested on an open charge of homicide. By the following year, Hassine was convicted of first-degree murder and began serving a life-without-parole sentence in Pennsylvania prisons.

While imprisoned, Hassine devoted himself to bettering prison conditions for himself and his fellow inmates and strived to promote prison reform through his written works of fiction and nonfiction. With others, he filed a conditions-of-confinement lawsuit at Pennsylvania's Graterford prison and joined another similar lawsuit after being transferred to Western Penitentiary. Combined, these lawsuits resulted in $125 million in improvements to inmate security and health care. Hassine also co-founded a post-release transition house for newly released prisoners who couldn't otherwise secure an acceptable housing plan, led a number of lifer's groups, and even founded the first prison synagogue where various religious services and educational programs were held. In 1990, for his continued efforts, Hassine received the Pennsylvania Prison Society's Inmate of the Year Award.

His dedication to improving prisons did not end there; Hassine is also an accomplished author of works on crime and punishment. He has been awarded many prizes from the PEN Prison Writing Program, which encouraged him in 1996 to publish *Life Without Parole: Living in Prison Today*, now in its fifth edition. In 2003, *The Journal of Applied Psychoanalytic Studies* published his essay, "How Do I Treat My Hungry Lion: A Model for Violence Management in Prison." Finally, Hassine is the major contributor to *The Crying Wall and Other Prison Stories*, published by WilloTrees Press in partnership with Infinity Publishing Company in 2005. Sadly, in April 2008 at the age of 53, Victor Hassine committed suicide shortly after being denied a commutation-of-sentence hearing.

ABOUT THE EDITORS

Robert Johnson is a Professor of Justice, Law, and Society at American University in Washington, D.C., and a widely published author. His social science books include *Culture and Crisis in Confinement, Condemned to Die, Hard Time,* and *Death Work,* which received the Outstanding Book Award of the Academy of Criminal Justice Sciences. Johnson has edited five social science books: *The Pains of Imprisonment, Crime and Punishment: Inside Views, Life Without Parole, A Life for a Life,* and *A Woman Doing Life.* Johnson has published extensively in professional journals (including law reviews) and has testified or provided expert affidavits before state and federal courts, the U.S. Congress, and the European Commission of Human Rights. Johnson's creative writing includes four collections of original poems, most recently, *A Zoo Near You,* and one anthology of fiction, *Lethal Rejection: Stories on Crime and Punishment.* His fiction has appeared in several literary publications. His short story, "The Practice of Killing," won a national fiction contest sponsored by *Wild Violet* magazine. His first novel, *Miller's Revenge,* was published by Brown Paper Publishing. Johnson is the Editor of BleakHouse Publishing, an independent literary press, and is a Distinguished Alumnus of the Nelson A. Rockefeller College of Public Affairs and Policy, University at Albany, State University of New York.

Sonia Tabriz, a J.D. candidate and merit scholar at The George Washington University Law School, serves as the Managing Editor of BleakHouse Publishing, an independent literary press, and the Editor-in-Chief of *Tacenda Literary Magazine.* Tabriz holds a B.A. in Law & Society and a B.A. in Psychology from American University, where she graduated *summa cum laude,* with University Honors, and as a member of Phi Beta Kappa. She received a variety of accolades during her undergraduate career, including the Outstanding Honors Student Award for three consecutive years and the prestigious University

Student Award for Outstanding Scholarship at the Undergraduate Level. Tabriz has also earned recognition for her creative work. Her short story titled "The Prison Librarian" (with Victor Hassine) and her poem titled "empty spaces" received Tacenda Literary Awards for Best Collaboration and Best Poem, respectively. Her short stories, poetry, and art have been published in several venues, including a collection titled *A Zoo Near You,* and a number of literary journals including *BleakHouse Review* and *Admit2*. Tabriz served as co-editor of *Lethal Rejection: Stories on Crime and Punishment,* an anthology that showcases a number of her original writings. Tabriz has also published works of general and legal commentary, including a law review titled "Death by Incarceration as a Cruel and Unusual Punishment when Applied to Juveniles: Extending *Roper* to Life Without Parole, Our Other Death Penalty."

PRISON

by Robert Johnson

Prison
life poisoning
punishment
for people of poverty

Prison
lash of rebuke
wielded like a whip
on the working wounded

Prison
dark black
dungeon of despair
denizen of the dispossessed

Prison
waste dump
for wasted lives,
house of refuge
for human refuse,
warehouse for
worn out,
used up
cast off
careworn creatures
now humbled and discarded.

Prison
time out
of sight,
time out
of mind,
for those
who don't
toe the line.

LIFE WITHOUT

Opening Reflections on Living and Dying in Prison Today

by Robert Johnson & Sonia Tabriz

Victor Hassine's *Life Without Parole: Living and Dying in Prison Today* takes the reader on a compelling journey into the hidden world of prison. The book draws on Hassine's personal experiences as a life-without-parole inmate, his social and historical observations of the prison world, and his literary talent for storytelling. Hassine's long life in confinement, spanning twenty-seven years and culminating in his suicide, is captured here in his own words and offers a thorough study and insightful commentary on prisons today.

Through his rich and varied observations and anecdotes, we come to know Hassine as a man struggling to forge and maintain a decent life for himself behind bars over many long years of confinement. He emerges as an astute observer who describes the lives and adaptations of other prisoners with empathy and insight, offering us a window into the underground world that is prison.

Hassine is, moreover, a thoughtful historian of the prison who relays a living history of prisons. His prison journey took him to a range of institutions, some old, some new, all menacing and demeaning in their own way. There is, in our view, no other book that allows us to appreciate a wide array of prisons in terms of their surface diversity and underlying uniformity. As a result, we are able to see beyond the physical and organizational differences of penal institutions to the core human experience they offer.

A writer of fiction, Hassine is also a gifted storyteller who uses vivid tales to convey essential elements of the human condition as they play out behind bars. In the compressed, high-stress world of prison, behavior is often couched in facades of toughness and false bravado that help prisoners survive. These veils of deception shroud important facets of prison life. Hassine uses fiction to uncover and reveal these hidden realities of prison life, sadly, the life he came to know best. Hassine felt strongly, and we concur, that his stories offer a valuable understanding of this underground world, and he wanted desperately for his readers to share these personal insights and appreciate them.

Hassine's ethnographic observations describe the prison world in commentaries faithful to his experiences and the experiences of the inmates around him. His short stories—"The Beast," "The Crying Wall," and "The Prison Librarian"—are original reflections on the issues that are central to his understanding of prison life. Read as a whole, this book examines prisons as living environments and takes us behind the scenes of prison life to take a closer look at the profound human drama that unfolds daily in prison, a remote and often alien world that is at the heart of our criminal justice system.

Victor Hassine was sentenced to life without parole in 1981 for capital murder. He was convicted of setting in motion a crime that resulted in a first-degree murder he himself did not commit. For 27 years, Hassine survived the harsh conditions of confinement in a number of Pennsylvania prisons, all the while embracing a rare but enduring hope for a better future, both for his fellow inmates inside the prison walls and for himself upon release. It wasn't until he was denied a commutation hearing that Hassine came to believe there was no escape for him—no possibility for release, no matter what he did. Soon thereafter, Hassine took his own life, hanging himself in solitary confinement on April 28, 2008.

Although he is no longer with us, Victor Hassine left the world with many small treasures in the form of his written works that give us a glimpse into the world that he had come to know so well. His thoughtful observations, insightful commentaries, and touching prison stories shed light on what our justice system is like now as well as how it ought to be and why. Hassine urges readers to contemplate the ways in which we design, build, and fill our prisons as he examines not only daily life as a prisoner but also the attitudes that shape our present-day policies and the implications of these policies for the greater society.

A large and growing number of offenders are sentenced to prison terms in America. When Hassine entered prison in 1981, there were approximately 340,000 male prisoners in American penal institutions. This amounts to an incarceration rate of 304 prisoners for every 100,000 free citizens. During Hassine's 27 years of confinement, the number of male prisoners grew to over 1.4 million, a dramatic increase in less than three decades' time that translates into an incarceration rate of 952 per 100,000.[1] Our incarceration rate, always high, is now astronomical by international standards; we imprison more of our citizens per capita than any other nation in the world, bar none.[2] Perhaps more troubling, our growing penal establishments increasingly house mentally ill offenders and deploy solitary confinement as a routine mode of punishment.[3]

Suicide is disturbingly common in our prisons, particularly among life-sentence prisoners like Victor Hassine who are uniquely vulnerable to the pressures of our increasingly cruel prison regimes.[4] This problem is likely to grow worse in the coming years. Our prisons house somewhere around 140,000 life-sentence prisoners, of which roughly 50,000 men are serving sentences of life without parole or its equivalent.[5] Lifers, the slang term for life-sentence inmates, accumulate like so much waste in our prisons. Few lifers eligible for parole are ever actually granted parole, and then only after decades of confinement; lifers ineligible for parole are only released in the very rare event of a commutation. (In Pennsylvania, where Hassine served his time, only 3 men of some 5000 lifers were commuted over a fifteen-year period.) The vast majority of life-sentence prisoners face, at best, a lonely death in confinement in their declining years. The statistics tell us that a disturbing number of them will turn to suicide.

Our relentless reliance on incarceration as a response to crime, together with our failure to address the underlying causes of crime, has produced American prisons that are overcrowded and underfunded, offering few amenities and fewer rehabilitation programs.[6] For today's life-sentence prisoners relegated to these grim human warehouses we call prison, the phrase "life without" captures assaults on their humanity so profound that outsiders can barely grasp them.

Lifers are, with rare exceptions, a class of living dead, persons sentenced to die hard, lonely, and often untimely deaths due to the traumatic stresses of prison life. More appropriately referred to as our other death penalty, prisoners serving life-without-parole sentences like Hassine undergo what amounts to "death by incarceration."[7] They are sentenced to die in prison. These inmates are not killed by an execution team, but instead experience shortened lives and painful deaths that are the result of the stressful and often debilitating conditions of prison life. Lifers do not live in prison so much as they live without—stripped of anything and everything that made them human, reduced to mere shells of their former selves.

Still, against the odds, prisoners, even lifers, often can and do hope for a better future beyond the cellblocks and prison walls. [8] Victor Hassine was one of these hopeful inmates saddled with a life sentence. Despite the dehumanizing circumstances of his life, he harbored hope for many years that somehow he would earn release, and he worked hard to prepare himself for the possibility of a meaningful life after prison. He read and wrote about what he experienced and witnessed, thoughtfully discussed the fundamental flaws and implications of the criminal justice system, tutored and mentored fellow prisoners, filed law suits on his behalf and on behalf of others (several successful), kept in touch with family, developed collegial relations with students of the prison (including the editors of this book), and maintained the hope that he might one day have a family and home and career of his own.

When those hopes were dashed by the vote of a board of pardons that would not even dignify his prison life and achievements with a hearing, Hassine appears to have assessed his life prospects and determined that all that remained open to him was a life behind bars. That life, it would seem, was simply too small for him. For Victor Hassine, and perhaps for other lifers, suicide offered a more dignified end than the daily round of cellblock and yard and menial labor, with free life always beckoning from somewhere just beyond reach, over the cold walls that frame so many prisons, holding the convicts inside and keeping the outside world at bay.

Victor Hassine is dead, but his life touched others in and out of the confines of the prison world. Through Hassine's tragic personal story and the compelling written works that bear witness to it, we learn that prison life revolves around three human sentiments: fear, loss, and hope. All men in prison are vulnerable and must live in fear. All men in prison are, in the final analysis, alone and apart from the larger society, and must live with loss. All men in prison, being human, cling to hope—for a decent day, a sustaining relationship, or, more ambitiously, a better life down the road, after prison. The roots of hope in prison are fragile. The arid soil of this lonely, frightening world provides little sustenance for the human spirit. Still, there is at times an almost palpable hunger for redemption amidst the bleak landscape of rejection that envelops prisoners, challenging them to keep hope alive.

HOUSE OF FEAR

The first major theme of this book and the prison experience is the pervasive and often raw fear that imposes itself onto almost every facet of life behind bars. Fear, we learn from Hassine's original short story, "The Beast," is a savage and sometimes cunning creature that takes many and varied forms. The prison can be seen as one giant cage, and somewhere in that cage a beast stalks its prey with a relentlessness that is matched only by its ferocity. Never knowing when or how it will strike, the beast leaves all the prison's inhabitants in a state of fear.

The wounded in prison are many, Hassine tells us, and the dangers of daily life—physical and emotional dangers that are either threatened or come to pass in acts of overt violence—must be lived to be understood. The reader is invited to enter the world of the beast on Victor Hassine's authority, and will be left with a vivid sense of the vulnerability and even sheer terror that haunts our prisons and can bring grown men to tears.

One salient source of fear is the threat of rape. Solid figures are hard to come by, but by any measure, prison sexual violence is disturbingly common and profoundly traumatizing.[9] More commonly, fear is generated by day-to-day conflicts that too often spark violence—interactions between rival gang members, a missed payment for washed laundry or illicit drug transactions, or even a simple look that was taken as a sign of disrespect. While homicide rates have dropped dramatically over Hassine's long tenure behind bars,[10] the raw, visceral fear of being threatened or attacked remained unchanged in Hassine's experience.

The prison is a dynamic social world for inmates and a somewhat cumbersome administrative structure manned by staff who are overworked, underpaid, and often disengaged from the inmate world. At bottom, the prison is a caste system—the bureaucracy holds great formal power (crucially, officials control who comes and goes) but in a sense the prison staff are merely visitors. It is the prisoners who live and die inside the walls in large numbers, who know the back-story of every encounter, who know what counts and who matters to their safety and well-being. But the prison, whether as home or work environment, has one underlying language, and that is the language of fear. Fear is the coin of the prison realm. Hassine and most other inmates ultimately adapt to prison and carve out a life for themselves, but they adapt against a backdrop of fear that can erupt into panic at any moment. Prisoners live like animals, relegated to cages with a savage animal in their midst—the beast, the specter of fear that lingers in the air, an ever-present feature of the prisoners' daily lives. If Hassine tells us anything in this fine book, it is that prison is a house of fear.

LIVING WITH LOSS

The second salient theme of Hassine's prison journey and personal life is the depths of loss inflicted daily in our prisons, captured in the poignant metaphor of a prison wall that weeps for the prisoners within, a wall that has held in its grasp the sorry lives of people discarded and abandoned by the larger society, a wall that has seen the workings of the beast and the maimed carcasses left behind and can do nothing other than mourn their hurt and loss. When you think of a prison wall, think of "The Crying Wall," the second work of Hassine's fiction. Prison is a constricted and constricting world symbolized by thick, high walls that keep prisoners in and society out, and limit daily life to a dreary, repetitive routine that spawns a deadening monotony that is a punishment in itself.

Loss in prison is constant regardless of time and place. Some prisons may be safer than others, but no prison has ever insulated its inhabitants from loss. As human beings, we derive a sense of purpose through our relationships; we develop a sense of significance, especially in our materialistic society, through the things we accumulate. It is no surprise, then, that prisoners undergo a profound sense of meaninglessness after being stripped of their tangible possessions and intangible connections to the outside world.

Life as we know it resides outside prison walls. A life inside prison is not a life, but a mere existence. Nowhere is the essential emptiness of prison life more obvious than in solitary confinement, sometimes called the Hole and always seen as a prison within the larger prison.

Victor Hassine ultimately chose to end his life in solitary confinement, a place that perhaps had come to symbolize the end of the line for him, the last stop in the prison world that had become his involuntary home and that offered him no escape other than his voluntary death at his own hands.

In drawing on the theme of loss, Hassine shows a kinship with the work of the classic nineteenth century writer, Fyodor Dostoyevsky, author of the famous novel, *Crime and Punishment* and the widely read prison story, *The House of the Dead*. Dostoyevsky used fiction as well as social commentary to reveal the hidden realities of his prison experience and expose the subtle, soul-crushing features of the prison life he endured. Slave labor and oppression by heavy-handed authorities were central features of the nineteenth century prisons Dostoyevsky observed; endless empty sentences may be more salient in the modern prisons Hassine has encountered. Putting those differences aside, Victor Hassine surely came to know, as Dostoyevsky had, the death of the spirit that is inflicted by prison—any prison, any time.

Every life story that leads to prison is a story steeped in vulnerability seasoned by loss; every feature of daily prison life, from the grim living conditions to the cruel lack of security in the face of violence, broadcasts how little we care about the prison's inhabitants. Prisoners are lost to the world. They have lost their claim to compassion and care. They have lost their sense of self worth, just as they have lost the people and things that made their lives worth living. Inmates, and especially lifers, are dead to the society that ships them off to be stored in human warehouses and then forgets about them.

PRESERVING HOPE

The last important theme developed in this book is hope, an increasingly improbable sentiment in the bleak world of the contemporary prison. Fear and loss lead easily to demoralizing despair. Some prisoners see the hopelessness of their situation from the outset, which is why entry into prison is a period of suicide risk for many prisoners.[11] New arrivals often are overwhelmed by the experience; they become despondent, dreading the possibility of living in this alien world.

Victor Hassine adapted in the face of great fear and loss, and was able to ward off the drift into depression commonly brought on by imprisonment. But even as he worked to achieve a life he could value, Hassine did not see much to be hopeful about in our prisons. This insight is particularly important because Hassine lived in many different penal institutions throughout his sentence, so many, in fact, that he is able to give us a natural history of the major forms prisons have taken. Throughout his prison journey, Hassine saw the best and the worst our prisons have to offer. He found little to recommend in any of them.

All that prisons do well, it would seem, is grow. And that growth, in Hassine's eyes, is a malignancy. Among Hassine's final entries, "The Runaway Train" is a troubling reminder of the way our penal system has run out of control, spreading invasively through the body politic, building a metaphorical wall between prisons and the larger society so profound that we seem at times to be a nation divided into convicts and keepers, with a huge supporting cast of criminal justice officials whose main job is sending people to prison or policing them upon their return.

This vision presents us with a dark depiction of the future, but the last thing Hassine wrote was "The Prison Librarian," a short story co-authored with Sonia Tabriz about hope born of healing human relationships and second chances. At some level, Victor Hassine saw himself as a man with hope for a free life of substance. He harbored hope; his family, friends, and colleagues supported him. That hope lived in him until the free life he so eagerly worked toward became unattainable. At that point, suicide appears to have offered Hassine a dignified escape from a life of endless captivity. Sadly, we know that many others are marooned in our prisons, holding on for dear life against terrible odds.

NOTES

1. The 1981 figures can be found at Table 1.7 (rate) and Table 1.6 (total). Snell, T. L. (1995) Correctional populations in the United States, 1993. *Bureau of Justice Statistics*. The 2008 figures can be found at Appendix Table 10 (rate) and Appendix Table 6 (total). Sabol, W. J., West, H. C., & Cooper, M. (2009) Prisoners in 2008. *Bureau of Justice Statistics, Bulletin*.

2. See Walmsley, R. (2003). Global incarceration and prison trends. *Forum on Crime and Society, 3*(1–2).
3. Often, mentally ill prisoners find themselves in solitary confinement because penal regimes tend to merge the concepts of "mad" and "bad" into one category: people who must be locked down for the smooth running of the facility. Toch, H., & Adams, K. (2002). *Acting out: Maladaptive behavior in confinement.* Washington, DC: American Psychological Association.

   "[T]he United States is one of the few countries [in the world today] that widely uses long-term solitary confinement." On any given day, as many as 80,000 American prison inmates are held in solitary confinement, many of them mentally ill. National Geographic Channel's Explorer: Solitary Confinement, http://channel.nationalgeographic.com.
4. Suicide is also more common among the mentally ill and among prisoners relegated to solitary confinement. Liebling, A. (1999). Prison suicide and prisoner coping. *Crime and justice: Review of research, 26,* 283–359. See also Tartaro, C., & Lester, D. (2009). *Suicide and self-harm in prisons and jails.* Lanham, MD: Lexington Books.
5. These prisoners are given a sentence of life without parole, one or more life sentences, or a sentence of so many years (we know of one sentence of 603 years, for instance) that it amounts to a term of life without the possibility of parole. Nellis, A., & King, R. S. (2009). No exit: The expanding use of life sentences in America. *Sentencing Project Research and Advocacy for Reform.*
6. Making prisons barren and uninviting—sometimes called "making hard time harder"—is an explicit goal of many American politicians. This includes federal politicians, who passed the revealingly named "No Frills Prison Act," limiting federal construction dollars to prison systems that cut back on a wide range of amenities and discontinued "good time," a practice that rewarded prisoners for good behavior by shortening their sentences. Johnson, R. (2008). Hard time: A meditation on prisons and imprisonment. In S. Nagelsen (Ed.), *Exiled voices: Portals of discovery—Stories, poems, and drama by imprisoned writers* (ix-xviii). Henniker, NH: New England College Press.

   In a thoughtful essay on American prisons, DeParle observed, "America's prisons are dangerously overcrowded, unnecessarily violent, excessively reliant on physical segregation, breeding grounds of infectious disease, lacking in meaningful programs for inmates, and staffed by underpaid and undertrained guards in a culture that promotes abuse." DeParle, J. (2007, April 12). The American prison nightmare. *The New York Review of Books.*
7. See Johnson, R., & Tabriz, S. (2009). Death by incarceration as a cruel and unusual punishment when applied to juveniles: Extending *Roper* to life without parole, our other death penalty. *University of Maryland Law Journal on Race, Religion, Gender & Class, 9*(2), 241–285.
8. This hope is tinged with an element of hard-won cynicism. Prisoners know that, in a way, all sentences are life sentences; criminal records are rarely wiped clean, stripping people of the chance to start a fresh life upon release. Prisoners are offenders or ex-offenders in perpetuity. Their records trail behind them, forming a kind of ethereal but durable simulation of a ball and chain. Even arrest records, which can reflect nothing more than accusations unsupported by convictions, can be crippling in our high-tech society, where everything recorded is permanent and virtually accessible to anyone.

9. "As three recent studies by the Federal Bureau of Justice Statistics show, prisoners are raped with terrible frequency in the United States. We still don't know exactly how many people are sexually abused behind bars every year, but we do know that the number is much larger than 100,000. And we know that those responsible for this abuse are usually not other inmates, but members of the very corrections staff charged with protecting the people in their custody." Stannow, L., & Kaiser, D. (2010, March 25). The way to stop prison rape. *The New York Review of Books*. See also Stannow, L., & Kaiser, D. (2010, March 11). The rape of American prisoners. *The New York Review of Books.*
10. See Mumola, C. J. (2005). Suicide and homicide in state prisons and local jails. *Bureau of Justice Statistics, Special Report.*
11. Suicide is more common in the early days of confinement and among long-termers as they age. See Liebling, A. (1999). Prison suicide and prisoner coping. *Crime and justice: Review of research, 26,* 283–359. See also Tartaro, C., & Lester, D. (2009). *Suicide and self-harm in prisons and jails.* Lanham, MD: Lexington Books.

1

In the Beginning

No matter how often I enter a prison I always experience a visceral, gut-wrenching reaction once I have stepped inside and heard the sharp, metal-against-metal report of the entrance gate slamming shut behind me. Even prior to my incarceration, when I routinely entered prisons as a criminal justice intern or law school graduate, the moment I was locked inside I experienced the same uncomfortable fear that I feel today as a prisoner, a fear that set in immediately after my arrest.

When I was arrested in 1980, I was transported by squad car to a local police station, an unimposing, two-story, white-washed cinder-block structure that included a lockup unit of less than twelve cells. The police lockup, commonly referred to as the "Drunk Tank," had no food service, clothing issue, or shower facilities and served only as a temporary detention facility for those awaiting booking and transfers to a city or county institution. Detention time in this lockup seldom lasted more than a few hours and was forbidden by Pennsylvania law to exceed twenty-four hours.

A police lockup is the initial entry into the American prison system and, by design, subjects detainees to a barely tolerable degree of captivity. In my case, I was unaware of the full impact of initial detention because of my preoccupation with my arrest. The public nature of the arrest process—flashing lights, loud sirens, and an overpowering paramilitary police presence—had me so frightened and confused that I simply did not have the emotional reserve to muster a response to being locked inside a cell. My solitary confinement in that cell actually afforded me some quiet relief from the distress and anxiety caused by the trauma of my arrest. By design or coincidence, the greater fear of arrest far outweighed the lesser fear of captivity.

To further quell resistance to the saddle of captivity, the entry process of local lockup is designed to allow detainees to feel as if they still have one foot planted in the free world. Although a Drunk Tank cell seems like any other jail cell, its surrounding environment still has the smell, touch, and unthreatening appearance of an office. During my stay there, I was able to entertain the notion that, despite my captivity, I was still free.

The Drunk Tank was air conditioned and well ventilated, so my nose was spared the smell of unpleasant odors. As I was the only person in the lockup, I did not have to deal with overcrowding or the sight of hostile, unfamiliar faces. The ceilings were low, the lighting bright, and the colors contrasting and varied. In the background were the muffled sounds of office activity rather than the roar of prison life. All these conditions helped to alleviate my fear of captivity. The fact that I was spared a strip search and allowed to wear my own clothes was perhaps the most significant calming factor.

After several hours in police lockup, I was transported to the Bucks County jail. This detention facility had the unmistakable appearance of a place that I absolutely did not want to venture into. Nicknamed the "Pine Street Motel," it bore the street-front appearance of a dark, ancient brownstone castle surrounded by a twenty-foot perimeter wall. This jail and prison held both pretrial detainees and convicts sentenced to less than two years of incarceration.

Handcuffed and flanked by two police officers, I was escorted into the interior of the castle. My perspiration and heartbeat increased as I penetrated deeper into the mouth of this monstrous prison, and I finally began to feel the mounting fear of my impending captivity. I sensed a change in the atmospheric pressure and humidity as I approached a rectangular cage of steel bars in the heart of the castle. This cage was the initial holding cell where all new arrivals, returns, or releases were collected, pending the processing of paperwork that would authorize their transfer to the prison population or release back onto the streets.

Several feet in front of the holding cage were the administrative offices, visibly in operation behind half walls mounted by transparent glass partitions. On opposite sides of the cage were half-lit corridors of mysterious doors and gates that greatly contributed to my fear, as I pondered their unknown purpose and destination.

Inside the cage were rows of long, narrow, backless wood benches worn smooth by decades of use and anchored to the dirty, concrete floor by steel bolts. Men in prison uniforms sat on these benches, eyeing my arrival with hard stares that unsettled me and invoked exaggerated imaginings of menacing, sadistic guards. I was convinced that I was surrounded by the most desperate, dangerous men on earth. Like myself, however, they were simply awaiting the processing of their paperwork.

Once inside the holding cell, the police officers who escorted me removed my handcuffs and disappeared behind the glass partitions. I sat on a bench farthest from the others, numb with fear, trying to collect my thoughts as I waited anxiously for whatever would happen next. For hours, I just sat there, watching and listening to the casual daily activities of prison life. Before me, convicts, prison guards, and policemen calmly and indifferently went about their business as if I were not there.

In this beehive of activity, the prison world around me seemed to grow larger than life, and I felt less and less significant, as if my identity was slowly being leached out of me. I imagined myself as some observer of a movie unspooling before me. This defensive detachment from reality, combined with the monotony of idle waiting, infused me with a sense of calm. Hence, I was able to rationally input and process information about my surroundings.

First came the visual image of captivity: dark, dirty, scarred floors and walls; dusty, dim lighting fixtures dangling from cathedral-high ceilings; shadows from poor lighting that made distant details hard to discern; a drab colorlessness and harshness to everything in sight; the steady flow of faceless strangers pouring in and out of corridors; the constant presence of stern, uniformed police and prison guards; and the unkempt, disheveled appearance of uniformed inmates. All these images were disturbingly unfamiliar. They were not only future signs of my fate but fixed environmental conditions that could not be escaped or altered. I felt hopelessly trapped.

Then came prison sounds to accentuate the severity of these images. A prison's "voice" is a cacophony of interminable, tortuous noises layered together at a constant pitch as pervasive as the air: loud, irritating, vulgar, and out of tune, all trapped by prison design and replayed as fragmented echoes throughout the prison.

The first layer of prison noise is a collection of constant mechanical droning from machines, motors, and engines. Layered over this is the higher pitch of sounds and voices from human activity. The final layer of noise—the loudest and highest pitched—permeates from a prison's operation: the intermittent slamming of gates, rattling of chains, and the screams of bells and whistles. This noise not only hurt my ears but also interfered with my normal ability to hear sounds that were important to me.

Like most built before the 1950s, the Bucks County prison had no ventilation system. Odors remained trapped inside until they found escape through open windows. Because the walls, floors, and ceilings consisted of porous stone or concrete, they were embedded with decades of decaying dirt, fungus, and bacteria that released putrid-smelling gasses to further foul the prison air.

Aggravating this condition were old, filthy mops used to clean floors, given that the Bucks County prison did not have a laundry system capable of routinely cleaning mop heads. As a result, mopping prison floors repeatedly every day to provide unskilled work to inmates actually increased the spread of dirt, fungus, bacteria, and odors throughout the prison.

Worst of all was the unmistakable stench of human waste. Like most prisons in the United States, Bucks County was overcrowded. At the time of my incarceration, in fact, it was about 300 percent over design capacity. Plumbing and waste treatment systems were grossly overtaxed and constantly broke down. On any given day, there would be an eruption of raw sewage or sewer gasses somewhere in the prison. This produced a nauseating smell that, combined with all other odors, created a noxious stench from which there was no relief. Though I eventually grew accustomed to the prison's odors, they still caused me great discomfort. At times when I breathed, I could taste the fouled prison air at the back of my throat.

My first tactile sensations on entering the county prison were the ambient temperature and the atmospheric pressure, both unique to this artificial environment. Because the Pine Street Motel was not climate controlled, heating and cooling was supplied by a primitive, inefficient system of cast-iron steam radiators and adjustable windows. The temperatures and atmosphere created by this air system were then trapped by the walls and ceilings of the prison.

Due to the county prison's massive building design and lack of air circulation, hot air would rise up to the tall ceiling area and force cold air down to the occupied spaces at ground level. On the unseasonably warm winter day of my arrest, the holding cage was chilly and damp. Had it been summer, the place would have been hot and humid. Only on temperate spring days, when all the windows were opened, would the ambient temperature be within the comfort zone. While I sat squeamishly in the holding cell, bombarded by frightening sights, sounds, and smells, I was shivering cold in my jacket and tie. The damp, clammy thickness of the interior's stuffy winter atmosphere nearly stifled my breath.

Despite my low-grade state of alarm, the long hours of waiting in the holding cell allowed me to settle down and feel more like my normal self. A prison's architecture of fear has its limitations: The longer I was submerged in the prison environment, the better my coping instincts adapted to it and enabled me to tolerate its fear-inducing agents.

The balance between the hostile environment and my fear management strategies was soon upset when I finally experienced the full force of the fear generated by the prison's administration. After my paperwork was completed, I became the official property of the prison staff. The district attorney had requested that I be transferred to the Philadelphia County prison, one of the oldest, most violent county penal institutions in the state and possibly the country. The law permits the housing of detainees in any facility, so long as it meets constitutional standards. Therefore, district attorneys often influence prison assignments to punish uncooperative defendants, often to encourage confessions or guilty pleas or to expose detainees to jailhouse informants.

Somehow, I never suspected anything sinister about my transfer. At this point, I was taken out of the holding cell by four officers and accompanied into a small bathroom. Crowded shoulder to shoulder with them, I was ordered to strip naked. The strip-search that ensued provoked a rush of overwhelming fear so distressing that I could actually smell the secretion of fear mingled with my sweat. More than anything else, this routine administrative procedure made me feel like an *inmate.* Two of the officers were Bucks County prison guards, the other two Philadelphia County sheriffs assigned to deliver me to the Philadelphia County Prison at Holmesburg. I was ordered to get dressed and then I was again handcuffed.

Thus began my transfer to Holmesburg, all performed with such dispatch and indifference that I knew with certainty now that I was nothing more than property—a prisoner of less importance than the paperwork that identified me. I remember thinking at the time that this transfer was to my benefit, because I was leaving a small, old jailhouse that looked, felt, and smelled like a dungeon, destined for a major cosmopolitan facility that certainly had to be less hostile. How wrong I was.

2

The Architecture of Fear

An outsider's knowledge of prison structures, rules, and regulations, no matter how comprehensive, reveals only what ought to be, not what is. To fully understand the prison experience requires a personal awareness of how bricks, mortar, steel, and the endless enforcement of rules and regulations animate a prison into a living, breathing entity designed to manipulate its inhabitants.

Prisons are uniquely designed to instigate fear in so many creative ways that fear has become a kind of language on its own, silently but relentlessly commanding specific inmate conduct and behavior. Prison designers and managers have developed a precise and universal alphabet of fear that is carefully assembled and arranged—bricks, steel, uniforms, colors, odors, shapes, and management style—to effectively control the conduct of whole prison populations.

Every time I look up at stacked coils of glistening razor wire atop fences around me, for example, I am being told, *DON'T TRY ANYTHING—YOU'RE SURROUNDED!* Fear is reinforced by the redundancy of steel gates and bars that warn, *THERE IS NO WAY OUT!* Unnecessary strip-searches and pat-downs that are repeated obsessively are actually reminders: *AT ANY TIME WE CAN DO ANYTHING WE WANT WITH YOU!*

The use of prison architecture to communicate fear and force to influence behavior is nothing new and certainly no secret. Consider the dark, powerful stone edifices and sinister, castle-like outlines of early nineteenth century prisons. No one would dispute that their foreboding exteriors were meant not just for security but as a warning: *STAY OUT OF PRISON!* Such Gothic-styled fortresses were designed to serve in part as menacing billboards to frighten people into obeying the law.

Surprisingly, even with this close, historic relationship between prison architecture and the communication of fear and force, the creators of these designs seldom if ever examined the provoking effects they have on the prison population itself. Consequently, their influence is rarely credited for a fight in the yard, a rape, a suicide, a riot, or, for that matter, even well-behaved inmates. Prison managers, therefore, freely explain away violent events as random or unique acts based on personal circumstances in an effort to avoid official responsibility for the fear-suffused environments they create.

The life-giving force of a prison is its inhabitants. Like blood, they course through the flesh and bone of a prison, stimulating its pulse. The nature of this pulse is established by the collective state of mind that exists within the prison population. Daily prison life is driven by the behavior of its inhabitants, whose actions are driven by fear. The amount of fear within its physical and operational body determines the mental state of a prison.

Holmesburg Prison was designed by the Quakers in the mid to late 1800s and reflected the *state-of-the-art architecture* of its time. The Quakers had earlier developed the concept of the penitentiary, expressed through the construction of Eastern State Penitentiary, the first one ever built. "Old Eastern," as the antiquated and now retired prison came to be called, was built in the vicinity of rapidly growing Philadelphia in the early 1800s. It continued to operate as a state institution until 1969, when it was finally closed and later converted into a museum. Holmesburg Prison, an offspring of Old Eastern, mirrored its design, purpose, and operation.

The Quakers made no secret of their belief that crime was the work of the Devil, operating through the acts of misguided humans. To these Quakers, lawlessness had to be discouraged by putting the fear of God into the hearts and minds of all those tempted to do the Devil's work. As a result, penitentiaries were designed to frighten and punish sinners, at the same time schooling them in the strict ways of righteousness. The fear and punishment components of the Quakers' penitentiary system were expressed primarily through architecture, while the religious programming component was accomplished through daily inmate management.

By nightfall, I was finally transported to the Philadelphia County Prison at Holmesburg, nicknamed "The Burg." Emerging from a squad car, I stood handcuffed and helpless before the old prison's monstrous, yet magnificent, dark stone walls. The gloom of that moonless night seemed to possess its stone and steel, awakening in me a sense of sinister foreboding.

Like many others in my circumstances, I would come to realize that confronting my fears meant abandoning the tillage of my past and the vistas of my future to address a present reality surrounded by threatening new possibilities. As the Burg's entrance gate slowly opened to swallow me up, I began to lose all hope with each step into the prison's belly. Only my fear and shame remained, guiding me through what I knew would be the worst, most terrifying ordeal of my life. With Old Eastern and The Burg, the "enlightened" minds of the nineteenth century had sufficiently mastered the alchemy of fear to reach out over a span of 150 years to frighten the hell out of me with their horrific creation.

The Burg was the shape of an octagon, at the center of which was a twenty-five-foot-tall, circular, single-story building with an arched ceiling, commonly referred to as the "center" or "control." Radiating out from the center were eight rectangular cellblocks, measuring about 450 feet long by 45 feet wide. These were circumscribed by a huge stonewall of 35 feet that connected to each of their outer extremities.

From an aerial view, The Burg resembled a gigantic spoked wheel with a rounded hubcap. Viewed from an outside street level, The Burg's many deflecting angles concealed its overall shape. The first time I saw the prison from this point of view, I was troubled by the fact that I could not fathom its appearance on the inside, as if confronted by a huge stranger wearing a mask.

Constructed entirely of dark stone, The Burg was a depressing world of grays and blacks, its bleakness magnified by an absence of windows. A primitive system of skylights served as the only source of natural light throughout the whole prison, each cell with one skylight and the center with a ring of them lining the rim of its ceiling. Electric lighting was another adverse factor. The inadequate number of light fixtures in The Burg produced a perpetual gloom of shadowy, colorless twilight. On my arrival there, this constant dimness not only deepened my depression but also obscured and distorted my vision, increasing my sense of vulnerability.

Throughout my five-month stay in The Burg, its collection of fear-inducing elements prevented me from a single peaceful night's slumber. It was always too cold, too hot, too humid, or too noisy to sleep.

The perpetual shadow world that surrounded me kept me nervously awake, worrying about unseen dangers lurking nearby. As a result, I remained irritable and confused due to chronic sleep deprivation.

The first time I ventured along one of The Burg's crowded walkways, it became fearfully apparent that if I were attacked by an inmate, no guard could possibly detect it or hear my cries for help. As a consequence of this glaring inability to police the cellblocks, I not only felt threatened but also frequently heard screams for help or witnessed violent attacks on these mobbed walkways. Once every newcomer to The Burg realized that prison guards could not protect them, it became necessary to seek one's own protection. The easiest, quickest, and most effective way to accomplish this was to form alliances with other inmates. The necessity of such alliances usually led to membership in a prison gang.

Under these circumstances, every act of inmate violence threatened a potential gang war. Predictably, The Burg served as an arena for the daily occurrence of multiple gang wars, varying in duration and degrees of violence. This fact earned The Burg the notorious distinction of being rated one of the country's most violent prisons, as well as the nation's capital of prison rape.

Everyone in The Burg, including the staff, was concerned about his or her own safety. Because prison guards on the front lines never ventured far from a cellblock's entrance gate, they rarely enforced the rules against inmate violence. As long as they themselves were not assaulted or endangered, all cellblock activity was negotiable, resulting in prison management by accommodation.

Such accommodations included allowing contraband into the institution, turning a blind eye to gang activity, and tolerating violence. Consequently, the response of guards to threatening situations was virtually indistinguishable from that of convicts. This behavior did not stem from corruption or greed but from a state of extreme, unrelenting fear that had made accommodation a necessary tool of survival.

The sights, smells, touches, sounds, and tastes of a prison are so terrifying that simply coming into contact with its physical components continues to have the most profound effect on my day-to-day conduct and behavior. These sensations also affect the way I feel about people and circumstances.

I have never fully overcome my fear of the prison environment, but I have managed to cope with it. However, this toleration does not include the fear generated by contact with the inmate population and the staff. Waking up every day to find myself completely surrounded by unreliable strangers and superficial friends, many of whom try to appear menacing and dangerous, is an extremely unsettling, stressful experience that has affected me deeply.

In addition to fears triggered by the prison's design and its inhabitants, I must cope with the crushing weight of its administration. Living under the thumb of an indifferent, punitive, arbitrary, and tedious bureaucracy with an obsession for rules and punishment is the stuff of nightmares. Furthermore, prison administrations strive to separate, alienate, humiliate, and minimize inmates, a process that greatly magnifies all other generated fears.

The Burg that I experienced during my incarceration was a world of daily administrative ignorance to extreme overcrowding, idleness, violence, and inmate self-policing. In essence, it was a crucible of violence, anarchy, and fear for both the keepers and the kept. My initial exposure to this old, dark, hostile, overcrowded institution was frightening enough. But once I realized that prison guards had tacitly ceded control of the prison to the toughest, most vicious inmates, my fear turned to panic. I found myself so terrified that the prospect of facing a capital murder trial seemed to be my least concern.

American prisons are virtual engines of fear, driving the conduct and behavior of everyone confined in them—staff and inmates alike. Criminal justice experts and the public at large generalize about prisons in terms of extraordinary incidents that periodically occur, such as rapes, assaults, riots, suicides, and murders. Relying on preconceived notions, they make assumptions and choose recommendations for prison management from a narrow understanding of prisons based on the sum of these incidents. In reality, such incidents account for a tiny portion of the drab, day-to-day prison experience.

Every aspect of prison life is measured and managed to prevent the occurrence of anything extraordinary. As a result, our prison is not simply a cage of stone and steel but an impermeable wall of rules and regulations grounded in fear and reinforced with hundreds of staff members specifically trained to make sure that we obey every rule.

To draw an accurate picture of prison life requires looking beyond its sensational occurrences and focusing instead on its dully oppressive, fear-suffused mechanical functions on a daily basis.

An honest examination of prison management would reveal that one of the great dangers of prison life is the maddening repetition of its daily routine. Too much reliance on routine can leave staff and inmates unprepared for the eventual occurrence of an extraordinary, sometimes violent event. A small minority of inmates undoubtedly needs to be restrained and controlled with strict, redundant, often dehumanizing fear. At the same time, responsible prison management should also address the following concerns: How do harsh, fear-generating systems affect the vast majority of well-behaved inmates; and do such systems, designed to correct a small minority, actually increase crime and violence within the greater prison population?

Surprisingly, the ubiquitous effects of fear-generating systems on a general population have never been studied to determine the change they produce in the majority of inmates. How prudent would it be if the medical profession suddenly required all its patients to take powerful, potentially harmful anti-cancer medication to treat the very few that might one day develop the cancer? Similarly, should prison managers be allowed to subject whole populations to the harsh, uncertain effects of artificially induced fear to prevent misbehavior and violence committed only by a very few inmates?

My experience has been that little occurs in a prison that is random or unique, and that nearly all extraordinary prison events and behaviors are common, predictable responses to the instigation of fear. Inmates are human beings who possess a biology, physiology, and psychology evolved from a keen sensitivity to danger, including the innate ability to manage or avoid things that frighten them. During my two decades or more of incarceration, little in my actions was not an instinctive response to the presence or absence of such fear within my environment. The multiple levels by which the prison world intrudes itself into my psyche have frustrated my efforts to initiate any thought or action that is not first filtered through these engines of fear. The overwhelming effect of a prison's many fear-based systems weighs so heavily on inmates that, in my view, it decisively influences their conduct and behavior years after they have been released from prison.

The combined effect of this constant fear and extreme idleness prevented me from ever fully adapting to the prison environment in The Burg. I was always too disoriented to think clearly. The Burg only released its inmates to the streets or to other state prisons. No matter what new environment they entered, however, most of them were still reeling from their previous habituation to extreme fear. After five months in The Burg, I was transferred back to Bucks County Prison to attend my trial. Even after I had been out of The Burg for weeks, I was unable to shed my fear, despite the more pleasant conditions in the Pine Street Motel.

3

Gauntlet of Despair

Graterford State Prison, Pennsylvania's largest and most oppressive penal institution, was built in the early 1930s to hold all of the state's most violent prisoners. I have heard Graterford called "The Farm," "The Camp," "The Fort," and "Dodge City," but I have never heard it called safe. When I was in the county jail awaiting trial, I saw grown men cry because their counselors told them they were being transferred to Graterford. It was a long timer's prison, most of its inmates serving sentences with minimums exceeding five years. At the time of my initial entry into Graterford following my conviction, it had the largest population of lifers in the state.

On June 14, 1981, while it could not contain all eight thousand or more of the state's most wanted, Graterford certainly had enough room to hold me. Its steel-reinforced concrete wall measures four feet thick by thirty-two feet tall and encloses over sixty-five acres of land. Originally designed to hold eight separate cellblocks within its perimeter, Graterford ended up with only five. However, these cellblocks are huge constructions, each containing four hundred cells.

Everything inside appears as huge and massive as the wall itself. Each housing unit is a rectangular structure, measuring about forty-five feet wide by three stories tall by eight hundred twenty feet long (over twice the length of a football field), perpendicularly attached to a quarter-mile-long main corridor that measures about twenty feet wide by two stories high.

I knew none of this as I sat handcuffed and shackled in the back seat of the sheriff's car, waiting to be taken inside to begin serving my life-without-parole sentence. All I could see was a blur of dirty, grainy whiteness from the giant wall that dominated the landscape before me. It made me feel very small and insignificant, and very frightened.

As I looked up in awe at the wall, the sheriff was saying something my mind couldn't process. I was distracted by fragmented recollections racing through my head—of my arrest, trial, the crowd of strangers who attended my sentencing, and my mother crying as I was led away for transport to this monster before me, opening its arms to me. These memories—uninvited, troubling—added to my fear, making it almost unbearable.

A giant steel gate rose up to allow the sheriff's car to drive into Graterford's cavernous sally port area, a fortified enclosure designed to control traffic. Once the gate fell shut, I was immediately hustled out of the car by some very large, serious-looking corrections officers. I knew I would have to submit to a cavity search, but it wasn't the strip-search that dominated my memory of this event. It was the *noise.*

Because concrete and steel do not absorb sound, the clamor and voices from within just bounced around, crashing into each other to create a hollow, booming echo that never ended. It sounded as if someone had put a microphone inside a crowded locker room with the volume pumped up, broadcasting the noise all around the sally port. It was this deafening background noise that would lull me to sleep at night and greet me in the morning for the next five years. Although I have been out of Graterford for many years now, its constant din still echoes in my ears.

The prison guards finished their search and escorted me up Graterford's dim, gloomy main corridor. They seemed distant, remote, almost unreal. Aside from their size, which was substantial, Graterford, like every other Pennsylvania prison I have been to, was operated by an almost entirely white staff while over 80 percent of the inmates were black. What was most striking about my escorts was their impenetrable air of routine and indifference. They were about to feed me to a pride of hungry lions as casually as if they were walking me through a park.

I was surprised to later discover that there was no open hostility between guards and inmates. As a matter of fact, I would come to see that many inmates and guards went out of their way to establish good relationships with each other. Inmates befriended guards in the hope that they would get such benefits as an extra phone call, special shower time, or the overlooking of some minor infraction. In turn, guards befriended inmates because they wanted to get information or just keep the peace and make it through another day without getting hurt.

The lack of natural light and the damp, dungeon-like air in this place was oppressive. As I took one tentative step after another, I promised myself never to take bright and sunny places for granted again. Having just left the courthouse hours before, I was so disoriented that I lost track of how far I had been walking.

Things changed dramatically and irrevocably once I reached the central corridor gate that separated the administrative section from the prison proper. This was the first time I saw the faces, shapes, and shadows of the men who would become my future friends, enemies, and neighbors. One man was staring menacingly at me, while another, displaying a row of broken and missing teeth, shot me an evil smile. Others seemed to stare right through me as if I had no physical form. They stared at me and I stared back, as scared as I had ever been in my entire life.

Once inside, I was walked through a gauntlet of desperate men. Their hot smell in the muggy corridor was as foul as their appearance. Most of them were wearing their "Graterford Tan," an ashen gray pallor. The discoloration of these distorted human forms represented the prison landscape. At Graterford you work, eat, sleep, and idle indoors. You never have to go outdoors unless you want to risk the sometimes-deadly yard. Many inmates served their time like cave dwellers, never leaving Graterford's concrete and steel shelter.

My first impression was that most of these men brandished their scars and deformities like badges of honor. None of them seemed to have a full set of front teeth. Many bore prominently displayed tattoos of skulls or demons. They all seemed either too tall or too small. None seemed right. Eyes were buggy, beady, squinted, or staring. None were caring. Heads were too big, too small, pointed, swollen, or oblong, some with jutting foreheads, twisted noses, massive jaws, and gnarled hands. None seemed human.

One could argue whether it was the look of these men that led them to prison or whether it was the prison that gave them their look. What tales of suffering their bodies told seemed to be of no concern to them. They were content to wear their scars openly like a warning, the way farmers use scarecrows to keep menacing birds away.

Today I feel pity and compassion for those who have had to suffer so much pain and tragedy in one lifetime. But on that hot June day, all I wanted was to get away from these ugly creatures as quickly as possible. Just looking at them made me fear for my life. There was no pity or compassion in my heart then, because their grotesque faces, bizarre dress, and tattoos made me forget they were human. Now when I watch a new arrival walking "the gauntlet of desperate men," I can always sense his hopelessness. I know my staring is as horrifying to him as it was for me on my first day, and I know what I must look like to him.

Toward the end of the main corridor I was shepherded into the shadowy expanse of yet another corridor. This led to the clothing room, a cold, damp place equipped with a tile-walled shower and an adjoining room where endless rows of mothballed clothes hung on racks like mismatched goods in a thrift shop. The eerie stillness and strong scent of old clothes made me feel as if I'd entered an embalming room. I shivered involuntarily.

My escort guard ordered me to "get naked" and surrender my personal effects to an inmate dressed in brown prison garb. I was still wearing my nice suit and tie from the courthouse. I hesitated, reluctant to surrender my clothes, my last ties to freedom. "Take your shit off," shouted the guard, "we ain't got all day!" I hurriedly stripped down, and handed the silent inmate the last vestiges of my social identity. He tossed them impatiently into an old cardboard box. After the guard conducted another "bend-over-and-stretch-'em" search, I was given delousing shampoo and ordered to shower.

The water was cold, the tiles on the floor gummy with dirt. As I stood naked and shivering after my shower, I was assigned two pairs of navy blue pants, two blue shirts, three T-shirts, three pairs of boxer shorts, three pairs of socks, a blue winter coat, a blue summer jacket, two graying white towels, and a pair of brown shoes. Everything but the shoes and socks had "AM4737" boldly stamped in black. This number was my new identity, as permanent as the ink in which it was written.

I dressed slowly, tentatively. Once I had dressed, I was taken to be fingerprinted and photographed, then escorted to E-Block, officially known as the Eastern Diagnostic and Classification Center. Although Graterford had five cellblocks, only A- through D-Blocks were considered part of the prison. E-Block was treated as a separate facility, which inmates and staff called "Quarantine." Because all new receptions, or new inmates, to Quarantine were issued blue prison uniforms, they were labeled "Blues." The general population inmates who wore brown uniforms were referred to as "Browns." Contact between Blues and Browns was strictly forbidden. Who was being quarantined from whom, I wondered idly.

Soon I found myself before the E-Block sergeant's desk, wearing my new blue uniform, cradling my belongings, and waiting for whatever came next. The sergeant walked me to a room full of bedding. There, another inmate in brown dropped a rolled-up mattress on my shoulder. Few words were spoken. Inside the mattress were stuffed a blanket, pillow, metal cup, plastic knife, fork, and spoon, a pack of rolling tobacco, soap, toothbrush, toothpaste, and a disposable razor.

Awkwardly balancing the mattress roll on my shoulder with one arm and carrying my prison-issue clothes with the other, I followed the sergeant down a flight of stairs to my cell on one of the bottom ranges. The moment I twisted my body and cargo sideways into the dark, narrow cell, the sergeant slid the door shut and disappeared from sight.

The next two days were spent in the prison's infirmary for shots and a complete medical examination. While it was a doctor who examined me, it was an inmate who drew my blood and wrote down my medical history. Because the infirmary was also used by Browns from general population, a guard followed me and the other receptions everywhere we went. This constant surveillance had me wondering why we were so heavily guarded.

I later learned that any exposure of Browns to Blues was closely watched by the staff. One reason was that, because they had more liberties than the new arrivals, Browns often tried to barter privileges with Blues. For example, a pack of cigarettes could buy extra phone time or a library pass; and for a pack a day, you could rent a TV or a radio. Also, some Browns would sexually exploit weaker Blues. Almost all of them were point men for prison gangs, who reported back on the new prospects among Blues for possible gang membership or future victimization.

After I completed the medical examination process, there were about two weeks of idleness. During this period all I could do was eat, sleep, and spend a couple of hours in a small and crowded mud-flattened yard. Boredom and monotony ruled my waking hours and greatly increased the value of the dreamless sleep that each night would rescue me, however briefly, from this torture. Finally I was taken to an examination room on the block for a series of written psychological and literacy tests. There was no supervision in this room, and the testing process took about two days.

Two months of more idleness followed as I waited to be interviewed by my counselor. There were over four hundred inmates on E-Block and many fights. It seemed as if every time the block was let out into the yard, a fight would break out somewhere. From my experience, when convicts are let loose after being locked up for long periods of time, aggressive behavior is an immediate and natural consequence. To occupy time, people played cards and worked out. It was during these idle days in classification that longstanding friendships and alliances were made, and when inmates distinguished the weak from the strong—predators from victims.

The first impressions I made on others during classification have stayed with me in prison ever since. Because I was not a career criminal, I was initially viewed as a "square john": a middle-class outsider with no experience of the social world of inmates. To both my advantage and disadvantage, I was seeing everything through the eyes of a foreigner, making many foolish mistakes yet gaining just as many unique insights into their world.

When I was finally called in for my interview, the counselor examined my test results and asked me a minimum of questions about my conviction and sentence. The interview took only ten to fifteen minutes. Two weeks later, I was summoned to appear before the classification committee. Sitting before a counselor, the block sergeant, and a major of the guards, I was asked what prison I wanted to go to and why. I could only suggest Graterford because I didn't think other prisons would be any better or worse. Then I waited outside while they reviewed my file. Within a few minutes, I was called back and informed that I had been classified to Graterford. Just before I left, the major added in a pleasant voice, "You'll be working for me."

At the time I didn't consider the significance of my job assignment. I was too relieved to know that the tortuous classification ordeal was finally over. A few days later, I traded in my blues for browns and moved off Quarantine into the general population.

To me and most of the others, as I later discovered, classification was a total waste of time. While different prisons in Pennsylvania purportedly provided different types of rehabilitation programs meant to serve the needs of various kinds of offenders, in reality it seemed that only three considerations were used to determine a convict's ultimate destination: (1) race, (2) hometown, and (3) availability of cell space. At the time, most of the minority inmates in the state were classified to Graterford or Western Penitentiary. The other seven prisons consisted of mostly white inmates under an all-white civilian staff.

From the inmate point of view, the testing was an utter sham. For one thing, the written tests were given to everyone without even determining who could read or write. The written tests I took were in an unsupervised room with about thirty other men, most of whom just picked answers at random or copied them from someone else.

Because the officials seemed flippant about the tests, inmates tended to see their results only as a tool of manipulation. Under this assumption, many men had developed theories on how to answer the test questions. Some felt it was best to copy from the brightest men to improve their chances at getting a clerk's job over kitchen or laundry duty. Others felt they should give lunatic answers so they could be medically released from work altogether. Still others gave no answers at all and faked illiteracy. Such men reasoned that they could enroll in school and appear to do extremely well, thereby fooling the parole board into believing they had worked hard to make a positive change in their lives. All these connivances were based on the inmates' understanding that they were being conned as much as they were doing the conning.

Inmates serving long sentences preferred to lock at Graterford because, even though it was violent, it afforded them the most personal liberty. This was because the more violent a prison is, the more reluctant guards are to enforce petty rules for fear of being assaulted.

Once I was classified to Graterford, I had to move my belongings, along with my mattress, blanket, and pillow, to B-Block. This was a working block, reserved only for those inmates who had been assigned a job. My assignment turned out to be a fortuitous clerical job in the major of the guards' office. All my belongings were fit into a single shopping bag that I carried in one hand, while my rolled-up mattress was once again toted on my shoulder. I walked down the long main corridor to B-Block, my new home. Although it mirrored the design of E-Block, it was considerably less crowded and noisy. Comparatively, this hell seemed more like heaven to me.

The first thing I noticed was that the men on B-Block were much older than most of those on the classification block. These were the "Old Heads" of the prison, inmates who had done a long stretch. When I arrived at my assigned cell, I quickly signed in at the block sergeant's desk and requested cleaning supplies. Then I spent the morning scrubbing down every inch of my cell. By noon count I was able to lie down on my bed, smoke a cigarette, and consider what I was going to do next.

My cell measured about six feet by twelve with a ten-foot-high ceiling, from which dangled a single light bulb with a drawstring switch. For furniture, I had a flat, hard steel bed and a steel desk and chair that had been assembled as one unit. The mandatory toilet afforded a sink directly above it with a steel medicine cabinet above that. High over the toilet was a rusty radiator that served as my only source of heat in the winter. Finally, I had a flimsy wooden footlocker with a hasp that could be locked with a commissary-bought combination lock—a commissary is a prison store, a bit like a corner market in a poor neighborhood. My cell entrance was a solid steel sliding door with a fixed glass window on the top quarter. On the opposite wall was a window that could be manually opened and closed, just a little. The concrete walls were painted a dingy off-white and adorned with graffiti and cigarette stains.

Despite the grim accommodations, this was home. I was due to report to work the next morning, and I could feel myself getting dug in. In prison it doesn't take much to make a man happy: food, some quiet, a good book, a job, and enough heat in the winter. That day I was happy just to be able to lie on that hard bed with a seventy-watt light bulb glaring in my face. I felt the worst was over. I could now begin to serve my time.

Like most first-time arrivals to Graterford, I was only preoccupied with survival and how to avoid becoming the victim of violence. This sudden refocusing of attention led me to change my habits, my personality, and even my values. With these changes came a new way of viewing the world as a place of unrelenting fear.

If I made eye contact with a stranger, I would feel threatened. An unexpected smile could mean trouble. A man in uniform was not a friend. Being kind was a weakness. Viciousness and recklessness were to be respected and admired. Oddly enough, these changes were in some way comforting. In the struggle to survive, it was easier to distrust everyone than to believe in their inherent goodness.

Danger became a determining factor of the changes in my attitude and personality. When there was general movement in the prison, for example, the main corridor would fill with hundreds of inmates in transit. This made the corridor an extremely dangerous place to be. I was more likely to see a stabbing than a guard on duty.

The cellblocks were just as insecure. A guard at one end of a cellblock could not identify anyone at the other end; the distance of seven hundred feet was just too great. Because of their fear of being assaulted where no one could see them, many block guards never patrolled the inner perimeter and spent most of their time avoiding conflicts at all cost, even turning the other way. I was on my own.

By the time I had settled in, however, I found myself feeling safe enough to think beyond the moment. This was something I had not been able to do since my arrest. Unfortunately, this new sense of security brought with it the "sleeping phase." I began to sleep twelve to fourteen hours a day. My whole life consisted of eating, working, and sleeping. I never dreamed. I only tried to stay unconscious for as long as I possibly could. I would imagine I was clinically depressed, although no one thought to examine or treat me, and I couldn't think of anything except getting through the day.

Although I had no way of knowing it at the time, I had entered a very common prison-adjustment phase. So common, in fact, that walking in on a newcomer while he sleeps is the most practiced technique of cell thieves and rapists. In Graterford, a man who spends too much time in bed sends the same signal as that of a bleeding fish in shark-infested waters.

"You can't be sleeping all the time," cautioned my chess partner one day, waking me to play a game. "You can't sleep away your sentence. In here, you have to stay awake to stay alive."

He was right, and I knew it. So I resolved to keep myself busy. I took up reading and painting as hobbies. I was allowed to buy almost as many books, magazines, and newspapers as I wanted, as well as canvasses, brushes, and paints. Self-help was encouraged so long as you could pay for it yourself.

Soon I was reading everything I could get my hands on and painting well into the wee hours of the morning. My cell became crowded with books, magazines, canvasses, newspapers, and even an easel. I went so far as to rig up extra lighting, hung pictures, and bought throw rugs for the cement floor. I had successfully transformed my cell into a cluttered boarding-house room.

Like some literary critic and master artist, I was so deeply submerged in my hobbies that I became as obsessed as a man digging his way to freedom. But I was no literary critic and certainly no artist. I was just another lifer trying to escape the real world.

"You have to spend more time out of that cell, Victor," insisted my chess mate and only friend at that time. "It's not healthy to do a 'bit' [time] like that. Look at your cell, you have junk everywhere. You even have lights on your wall that look like they belong in a room somewhere else."

"I'm just getting dug in," I replied in defense, annoyed that my efforts at avoiding reality had been detected.

"This isn't getting dug in, this is foolishness. You're in a penitentiary—a tough one. You should never try to forget that. Never try to make yourself believe you're somewhere else. Do you know what a lit match could do to this cell?"

His words struck an unnerving chord. Only a few months earlier, I had watched a man whose cell across the way had been deliberately set on fire. He had screamed and banged helplessly on his locked door, flames dancing around him, biting at his flesh. Through his cell window, I could see billowing black smoke envelope his pleading, twisted, horrified face until he disappeared. It had taken some time before guards responded to his screams. The very next day I gave away my books, magazines, newspapers, art supplies, and easel. I knew I had to fight as hard for my safety as I did for my sanity. I still hear that man's screams sometimes, when I have trouble sleeping.

4

Staying Sane

I never considered that my mental health was in any peril because I focused all my attention on trying to keep myself physically intact. Only after I had overcome the physical dangers of prison did I discover the greater challenge of maintaining sanity. In truth, the American prison experience includes a slow, steady regression toward the threshold of madness.

Most convicts manage to survive this ordeal, but none remain unscarred by it. Those fortunate to outlive the physical prison find themselves thrust inexorably into the greater struggle to overcome the psychological prison. American society, which always values the mental health of its citizens, should be more concerned about a criminal justice system designed ultimately to drive millions of its incarcerated population insane.

My introduction to prison-induced madness came in the form of Cherokee, one of Graterford Prison's most esteemed inmates. When I first arrived there in 1981 to begin serving my life sentence, Cherokee had already been incarcerated for more than forty years. At some time during his long imprisonment, the Graterford staff ceased treating him like an inmate and elevated him to what amounted to the status of a mascot. To the inmate population, he was as ingrained into Graterford as its bricks and mortar. But whether anyone considered Cherokee a mascot or a fixture, neither description seemed a fitting way to view a gentle human being who for forty years did nothing more than exactly what the administration expected of him.

When I first met Cherokee, he was scavenging inside a fifty-five-gallon drum of prison trash. As I stood beside it, he took me off guard when he surfaced with a handful of pickings. Having lived in New York, I was unsurprised by the sight of a man mining refuse and paid little attention to him. Gripping a load of garbage, Cherokee produced a huge smile and quickly placed his catch into a large plastic bag.

"Hey there, you must be a new fellow," he addressed me politely. "My name's Cherokee." He stood over six feet tall, sporting a pot belly bulging from his worn, faded brown prison uniform. His hair was a dingy yellow like wind-blown straw, with streaks of white and gray, and his yellow teeth matched the color of his hair. His friendly, gentle tone obliged a response.

"My name's Victor," I replied.

His puffy cheeks swelled, as his smile broadened. "We don't get many Victors in here," he offered pleasantly. "You look like such a nice young fellow. You don't look like you belong in here." From that moment, Cherokee became my friend for life.

The big man gazed down at his bag of goodies and said, "You'd be surprised how much good stuff I find around here, like cups, and shoes, and socks. Once I found me a pretty good coat. Wasn't nothing wrong with it. I gave it to another young fellow who didn't have one to wear." Then he chuckled, "You young folks today sure like to throw things away."

I returned his smile and nodded, as he continued. "I give a lot of stuff away to anyone who needs it. You know how fellows can get down on their luck in here. So, if you got anything you want to throw out, you be sure to let old Cherokee know. And you don't have to worry about me, I'm okay. Everybody knows me. Just ask anyone about Cherokee."

He picked up his bag and lumbered off toward the next trash drum, also overflowing with garbage. After a few steps, he stopped and turned. "Oh, did I tell you I collect stamps? If you get any, I hope you'll give them to me. I'll stop around your cell." Cherokee and his bag moved on without looking back.

Throughout my stay at Graterford, I saw Cherokee frequently. Usually, he was digging his way into or out of a trash can or a dumpster. Sometimes, he would stop by my cell and ask if I had any stamps for him. I would give him all the canceled letter stamps I had received, and this seemed to make him very happy. Once in a while, I offered him some cigarettes, candy, or coffee, but he refused to accept anything, as it somehow interfered with the intention of his visit. Soon, I was storing commissary items in a brown bag for his next visit. He always took the offering, never saying a word. His smile was all the thanks I needed.

Cherokee's demeanor suggested that he no longer recognized his surroundings as those of a prison. His unique behavior was not what set him apart from all other inmates but rather the way the prison staff treated him. He was allowed to run free in the prison so he could forage anywhere he wanted. His only requirement was to return to his cell for count; his cell usually only locked at 9:00 pm. He needed no pass to go anywhere and could visit the kitchen at any time, eating anything he liked. Staff members often gave him candy bars and snacks purchased from an employees' vending machine. No inmate dared say an unkind word to Cherokee, because both guards and prisoners were fiercely protective of him. In a maximum-security prison, this kind of high status was rare and extraordinary.

I did not give any of this much thought at first and assumed that such long-toothed seniority entitled Cherokee to special consideration. After all, forty years of captivity had turned him into a harmless old man who was kind, likeable, and unlikely to escape even if the prison walls came tumbling down.

My suspicions of this apparent altruism toward Cherokee grew after I met other convicts who had served as much or more time. The institutional policy was to treat long-timers the same as other inmates, with no special consideration or privileges. I kept wondering why Cherokee had been singled out to receive the benefit of the staff's mercy and kindness. If prison managers wanted to do the decent thing for Cherokee, they would have sent him to a minimum-security prison or helped him to get a commutation of his sentence, so he could be committed to a nursing home. At the very least, they could have provided him with some mental health care. Allowing this harmless old man to live out his life rummaging in prison trash cans did not reveal any real decency—it was actually a form of degradation and humiliation. I eventually came to understand that Cherokee's privileges were not meant to benefit him but to advance the prison's interest in displaying a "model inmate."

For forty years, Graterford had invested money and resources to hammer, bend, fold, and shape Cherokee into the mold of rehabilitation. The old convict was now obedient, functional, low maintenance, dependent, and virtually harmless. What more could prison management want? It made no difference that in the process of conditioning him into a model inmate, Cherokee had been driven to quiet madness. He had to be punished for his crime, and apparently forfeiting his sanity was a fair price to pay. This was Graterford's brand of mercy and redemption.

What the prison staff passed off as acts of kindness were actually inducements for others to conform their behavior to that of their model inmate. Certainly, staff members were genuinely fond of Cherokee; but in a prison, fondness must always stand a distant second to control. Cherokee, first and foremost, was a helpless, unwitting tool in a prison's long-term effort to achieve absolute control over the inmate population.

Anyone who has not felt the pinch of prison shackles will likely scoff at the notion that a modern governmental bureaucracy would knowingly induce insanity to maintain control. But consider this: if you were the warden of an overcrowded prison plagued with violence, corruption, drugs, disease, and lack of resources, Cherokee's smiling figure emerging from the trash to greet you might make you wish that all your inmate charges could be as respectful, obedient, and well-behaved as this old long-timer.

Finding the time and place to be alone in a prison is almost an impossibility. Overcrowding has seen to that. Whenever I discover an opportunity to be by myself, I try to exploit it. One hot summer day during my incarceration, the heat was so oppressive that none of the other inmates dared to venture out into the small area of dirt and dust shamelessly designated as the "recreation yard."I was desperate for some privacy within the walkway area running between the new housing units that now replaced the old main yard. This area had no grass, no space, and no room to exercise. All that existed was a long, crooked concrete walk flanked by parallel strips of dirt with bleachers intermittently installed wherever they would fit.

Finding any unoccupied space under these circumstances was normally a ludicrous undertaking. But on this day, thanks to the stifling heat and burning sun, the yard was completely empty. I hurried to a remote spot to sit on one of the scorching bleachers, a small price to pay for privacy. I closed my eyes and ignored my discomfort as I drifted off into my own thoughts.

Before I had a chance to fully appreciate my solitude, I was startled by a tap on my shoulder, along with an urgent voice: "Victor, I need to talk to you."

Under normal circumstances, I would have ignored the intruder, but the voice belonged to Kareem, one of the more respected, honorable convicts in the institution. He was a prison gangster who took no nonsense from anyone, but he was also a fair and reasonable man who only challenged those who tried to interfere with his space.

Hearing the urgency in his voice, my eyes immediately sprung open and my mind instantly focused on the possibility of danger nearby. "What's going on, Kareem?"

Kareem must have detected my concern, as he lowered his voice. "No, there ain't no trouble. I just need to talk with you about something personal." He moved next to me on the bleachers and sat down in the burning sun.

"What's going on?" I was a bit annoyed, but he had piqued my interest. Kareem was not the sort to waste anyone's time.

"I'm going crazy, Victor, I'm losing my shit," he blurted out, his eyes hawkishly searched our surroundings.

"What do you mean?"

Kareem's dark brown eyes fixed on me, wide and piercing. "I've been hearing voices. I know they're not real, but I hear them anyway."

What could I say? Prison life has taught me to be prepared for anything, so I collected my thoughts and asked calmly, "What do these voices say?"

"They tell me to do stupid stuff. You wouldn't believe it. I don't do any of them. I just hear the voices."

My curiosity rose, as I realized I was talking to a man on the verge of a mental breakdown. "Yeah, prison can make anyone hear voices. It's a shame what they do to a man in here."

"Ain't that the truth," he answered, sounding relieved that I understood his problem. "I've seen lots of Old Heads lose their shit, but I never thought it would happen to me."

"Well, maybe it's just a temporary thing and will go away," I suggested. "You're a strong man. You can beat this."

"No, man, I don't think so. I can feel myself slipping in and out. I tried to fight it a couple of times, but my mind just keeps snapping—I'm just going crazy." He added a chuckle to that.

"What do you think brought this on?"

"Nobody in my family's crazy—it has to be this prison. The time is getting to me. I've been doing this bit for a long time."

Kareem had served over twenty years of a life sentence, and his prison escapades had made commutation less than a remote possibility. For a moment, I reasoned that perhaps he was a drug abuser whose mind had recently surrendered to his addiction. I worried about whether a similar fate might await me as my life sentence unfolded.

As if hearing my thoughts, Kareem added, "All my life I've avoided drinking and doing drugs because I'd seen what it did to other people. Now look at me anyway."

"I don't know what to tell you, Kareem. Sane or insane, these people want their time out of you. You're going to have to fight this thing."

"You know, I've done a lot of time in the Hole. When I started my bit, I didn't care nothing about going to the Hole. But these last few times, they were real rough."

"What happened in the Hole?"

"Nothing this last time, but just being down there with these guards messing with you and all that time alone. I think I started slipping while I was in the Hole."

"Did you hear these voices in the Hole?"

"No. I just started hearing them. When I was in the Hole, I didn't hear nothing. I'm not good with reading, so I just sat in my cell sleeping and thinking."

"You think the Hole made you crazy?"

Kareem thought for a moment. "No. I don't think it was the Hole alone. I think it's everything put together. You know, doing time ain't no joke."

"No, it isn't," I agreed.

"And you know what's the most amazing thing about all this?" He suddenly took on the animation of a child, eager to share a secret. "The way it just kind of crept up on me. One minute I was normal, the next minute I was bugging out in my cell, talking to myself. I didn't know going crazy could snatch me from behind like that."

A long silence lingered between us, both of us lost in our own separate thoughts.

"You're doing a life bit too, aren't you?" Kareem asked.

"Yeah, I got eight in and it's killing me. I can imagine how you feel."

"No, you can't, and you really don't want to." He reached out with his hand as if grabbing at something in the air. "Don't you worry about any of these motherfuckers messing with you. You just make sure you hold on to your mind. Don't let these people sneak up behind you and snatch your shit."

As he stood up and left me alone on the bleachers, Kareem's last words echoed back to me: "Nobody deserves to be treated like this. They might as well have killed me." Suddenly, I did not feel much like being alone anymore.

5

Things Missed

One of the more subtle ways a prison punishes is by its neglect of a man's need for things, both the abstract (e.g., his freedom, his sanity) and the tangible (e.g., his personal property). From the very start, I began missing both. Just when I would get accustomed to doing without old things, I would start to miss new things. Once I had gotten accustomed to doing without things, I would start to miss different free-world things. It was a selfish, childish, material missing that somehow kept me rooted in my pre-incarceration past by having me constantly remember and mourn those lost objects and things that had once represented the liberty I'd lost. It was almost as if prison life had created a newfound desire in me to miss something all the time.

At first, I missed the obvious: sex, love, family, and friends. This left me feeling sorry for myself. But it wasn't long before I stopped missing these things and started focusing on the next wave of things I no longer had: privacy, quiet, and peace of mind—intangibles that I have never stopped missing to this day. At least these things I could try to find in prison, or some version of them.

There are no trees in the great walled fortress of Graterford and very few shrubs. In fact, there isn't much of anything green that hasn't been painted green. Also, the prison is designed so that you can never get an unobstructed view of anything. Walls keep getting in the way. Occasionally when I had to make trips outside the prison for court appearances or doctors' visits, I would sit in the prison van enraptured by the trees whizzing past. The brightness and the beautiful colors of everything around me made every outside trip an exciting experience. I know of several men who filed lawsuits or feigned illnesses just to get a moment, even so brief, out of the prison and see "some streets."

Well aware of this, the administration would try to make such trips as uncomfortable as possible. They would handcuff and shackle traveling inmates and strip-search every man coming and going, even though he never left the sight of an officer. They would make certain that an inmate wore ill-fitting clothes that were dirty, torn, and extremely uncomfortable. In the winter they had only summer clothes available and only winter garments in the summer. For a while they even required a man to be locked in his cell the day before making such a trip.

But no amount of discouragement worked. Inmates loved these trips because they reminded them of all the things they missed. Personally, I always came back from each trip remembering the trees, the beautiful women, and all the joys of the outside world. Longing for these things made me take a lot of risks in my efforts to reclaim even the most insignificant of things that I once had taken for granted.

My first misconduct at Graterford resulted from missing one of life's simplest pleasures: a fresh-cooked, juicy hamburger. I had just started working the 12:00 to 8:00 pm shift as a clerk in the major of the guards' office, which was off the main corridor between E- and D-Block. One day a contraband sandwich merchant, or "swag man," walked into the office and offered me a ten-pound bag of frozen ground beef for a pack of cigarettes. I had no way of cooking it, but for another pack I could get a hot plate. I began to imagine myself biting into a hot, juicy burger grilled to perfection. I bought the contraband beef, which was a bargain considering that a pack of cigarettes at that time cost only fifty cents in the commissary.

A senior clerk helped me out by talking to an inmate kitchen worker, who quickly produced the heating element of an electric coffee urn and an aluminum cookie pan, both hidden in the lining of his oversized prison-issued coat. For only one more cigarette pack, he scrounged up hamburger buns, chopped onions, butter, sliced cheese, ketchup, mustard, and two bricks to hold the cookie pan over the heating element.

That evening when the meat had finally thawed, my co-conspirators and I set up a makeshift grill in the major's bathroom. We fashioned burger patties and started frying the hamburgers as soon as movement in the main corridor had ended.

It was the onions that did us in. The aroma of sautéed onions in butter was so strong that it attracted a guard stationed some three hundred feet away. He followed the aroma to its origin and asked us for a burger. We were more than happy to share with him, and he was eating it as he left the office, which made us all sigh with relief.

A few minutes later, a Search Team raided us and confiscated everything. They had been tipped off when the previous guard offered one of them a bite of his tasty burger. When they asked him where he had gotten it, he simply told them. Apparently the members of the Search Team were not as impressed with our resourcefulness.

In the early 1980s, Graterford introduced the Search Team, or "A Team," as a special two-man guard squad whose sole function was to conduct cell searches and pat downs. Not even the block officers knew who or when they would strike. Whenever a Search Team entered a block, an inmate would call out, "Search Team up!" Inmates at the end of the block would immediately hide their contraband. Because it took so long for the team to make it down the long block, contraband was moved constantly without detection.

Given that our hamburger caper took place in the major's office, however, we didn't have that advantage. We were all issued misconduct reports for the possession of contraband. Following a misconduct hearing, I was found guilty, removed from my job, and forced to pay for the food. I was also confined to my cell for sixty days, allowed out only two hours per day for recreation on the block.

My biggest mistake in this case was my naiveté. Until the Search Team had confiscated the burgers, I thought that such activity was merely business as usual at Graterford. I had only been in general population for about a month, and things developed with such effortless ease that I hadn't taken what I had done very seriously. For many years afterward, my prison handle became "Burger King," even though I had never gotten a chance to taste the object of my crime.

The foremost tangible things missed by inmates are their stolen personal possessions, particularly considering how little they're permitted to keep in their cells. At Graterford, there was always an epidemic of cell thefts. Fortunately for me, everybody on B-Block where I lived had jobs. This meant that most of them made enough money to shop at the commissary every week.

Some of them had manufacturing jobs in Correctional Industries, such as weaving, shoemaking, or tailoring, and could make well over a one hundred dollars a month if they worked overtime. By prison standards this was considered a small fortune. Total employment meant that there was not a major theft problem on B-Block at the time. This was a great relief to me, not because I didn't expect to get some of my things stolen, but because I didn't want to deal with the inevitability of catching some thief in the act.

In the life of an inmate, if you catch someone stealing from you, you're compelled to deal with it physically. This is not because you want to or you think it's the right thing to do, but because you absolutely must. If someone steals from you and you decide to report him to the guards, all that will happen is that the thief will go to the Hole for a while. Soon he'll be back in population and ready to seek revenge.

Revenge in prison can take place years down the road. It generally occurs when you are vulnerable and the avenger happens to be around. This reality will leave you constantly looking over your shoulder. In addition, involving the guards will get you the reputation of a "snitch," which means you will be physically challenged by inmates seeking to make a reputation or pass their own "snitch" label onto you.

If you choose to ignore the theft, the man will steal from you again and tell his friends, who in turn will also steal from you. Eventually, you will be challenged for more than just minor belongings. This "Inmate's Dilemma" is precisely why most men in prison hope they never have to deal with a sloppy cell thief. Unfortunately, many men who were caught stealing on the streets will just as easily get caught stealing in prison.

In 1982, there was no way an inmate could lock his own cell at Graterford. Cells were all locked or opened simultaneously at given intervals by the pulling of a single lever. At 6:00 am, for example, all the cells on the block were levered open so each inmate could open and close his own cell during breakfast. Five minutes after last call for breakfast, the levers were pulled again to lock all the doors. If you returned late from breakfast, you would have to wait for all the cells to be levered open again before you could re-enter your cell. In case of an emergency, each guard had a key that could override the lever and let you in. But asking a guard to key you in was like asking for a key out of the prison.

This process of opening and closing all doors at once was repeated at 8:00 am for work lines and yard line; then again at 11:00 am for count; at noon for lunch; at 5:00 pm for count; at 6:00 pm for supper; at 6:30 pm for block out, yard out, or work lines; then finally at 9:00 pm for final count and lockdown. Every one of us religiously followed this schedule because we always wanted to be at our cells when they opened up. Otherwise, we stood the chance of losing everything of value.

To combat theft, I arranged a neighborhood-watch system with my neighbors to look out for my cell when I wasn't there and vice versa. But for the most part it was every man for himself. From time to time I would return to my cell and discover things missing. Any theft was an intrusion into "my space" and made me angry. My few personal belongings constituted my total worldly possessions so they were of great (probably inflated) personal value to me. I was also left frightened by the threat implied by someone taking something of obvious value to me. Fortunately I have never had to face the Inmate's Dilemma, but many others have and the consequences were brutal.

There is no walking away in Graterford—the walls see to that—so either the intruder or the victim ends up seriously hurt. One example of a cell confrontation involved not a cell thief but a peeping Tom. One of my cellblock neighbors was Dip, a cocky bodybuilder with an imposing physique. He was convinced that the mere sight of his impressive frame would deter anyone from ever messing with him. While other inmates ran to their cells when the levers were thrown to protect their belongings, Dip never bothered.

Then one day Dip returned to his cell from a shower, wearing only a towel around his nakedness. To his shock, he found an inmate hiding under his bed with an exposed erection, trying to watch him undress. Dip was so caught off guard that the intruder simply walked out, blowing him a kiss as he turned to run off the block. Once he had recovered his senses, Dip got very mad. He dressed himself for combat and stormed down the block to find the man who had challenged his manhood. The jeers and heckles of neighboring inmates only served to deepen his rage.

But the moment Dip stepped into the main corridor, the kiss blower was waiting with some friends. Dip was stabbed several times with homemade knives. Lucky for him, his injuries were only "Graterford wounds," meaning that his vital parts were still intact. By the time guards had made it to the scene, the attackers were gone, one of their knives was left behind, and bleeding Dip was locked up—charged with possession of the weapon that had been used to stab him.

For the most part, the prison administration did nothing to curb cell thefts or invasion of cell privacy. Some guards also seemed to think that these thefts and intrusions were part of the punishment of prison. In due time, however, the administration's failure to provide adequate safety and security would have far-reaching consequences.

Throughout 1981 and 1982, inmates petitioned, begged, and even threatened in their efforts to convince the administration to provide some means by which inmates could lock their own cells. The administration rejected these requests, claiming that cells were secure enough. If the administration had conceded to such requests, it would have been a tacit admission that they did not have control over their own prison.

By 1982, Graterford's general population rose to over two thousand. Every cell in the general population blocks was occupied and in the classification block the new receptions were already being double-celled. There were not enough jobs to go around now, so many men sat idle on B-Block. This resulted in more theft, which in turn led to more fights and more stabbings.

As thievery increased, gangs flourished. Some gangs were formed to steal, others to defend against burglaries and robberies. Because B-Block comprised mostly working inmates, the fighting was not as frequent. But C- and D-Blocks were virtual war zones. There were so many fights and retaliations that guards were getting injured in the melees.

Only then did the administration take action. Holes were drilled in the cell-door tracks so that any cell could be locked from the outside with a padlock, even when the master lever was opened. The commissary began selling padlocks that could fit in the hole. There was a general feeling of relief because now we could secure our belongings. It seemed less likely now that we would ever have to deal with the Inmate's Dilemma—or so we thought.

Once gangs form in a prison, they're hard to break up. When a group of cell thieves join together, no lock can stop them. Their incentive had increased now as well, especially because this new sense of security encouraged inmates to keep more valuable goods in their cells.

To get around the new cell locks, thieves simply changed their techniques. The problem that remained was that when the master lever was open and the inmate was inside his cell, he could not lock himself inside the cell. Instead of waiting until an inmate left his cell, a gang would simply rush into the cell while he was sleeping or using the commode. This resulted in even more fights and stabbings.

Burglary is one thing, but strong-armed robbery demands an immediate and violent response. As the number of robberies and assaults surged, the new jailhouse wisdom was that you should always be awake and ready to fight when cells were opened, and that you should use the commode only when your cell was locked.

Some prisoners began fashioning weapons that could withstand a shakedown. For example, they would keep wooden floor brushes in their cells. Made of solid oak, these heavy brushes could knock a man unconscious. Because they were prison issue, they weren't considered contraband. If a guard found one in your cell, all he could do was confiscate it or order you to return it to the block sergeant. Ironically, the heavy-duty combination locks sold in the commissary served as another shakedown-proof weapon. Placed in a sock, this weapon could be more effective than most homemade knives.

The ultimate defense against unwanted intruders was getting a hole drilled on the *inside* of your door. A bolt secured in this hole prevented the door from being opened, so you could now lock your cell from the inside as well as from the outside. The staff objected to this hole on the grounds that an inmate could barricade himself in his cell so it could only be opened with a cutting torch. If a guard saw a hole on the inside of your door, he might plug it up with metal solder, but it was easy enough to get another hole drilled.

A combination lock on the inside door-jamb hole rendered a man's cell fairly secure. The ability to keep more property without being restricted to their cells freed inmates from the routine of protecting their belongings. This meant more socialization, recreation, and work. It also meant the gangs would have to change their style of doing business once again. The treasures now accumulating in the cells were just too much to resist.

6

Playing the Opposites

Shortly after I arrived at Graterford, I discovered that my fellow inmates made a point of "playing the opposites." This game involves reverse psychology, where prisoners state the opposite of their actual feelings when asked by someone in authority to voice a preference or an opinion. A common occasion for playing the opposites is when an inmate is being interviewed by a counselor or employment officer for a job assignment. Naturally, some work details are favored over others, so experienced inmates will do whatever they can to secure a desirable job.

Some inmates will state their real job preferences and then try to influence assignments by summarizing their qualifications. This approach occasionally succeeds, but only if the convict possesses some unique skill currently in demand. As a general rule, inmates don't receive the jobs that they request. Consequently, a more savvy convict won't hint at his preference; instead, he misleads the staff member into believing that he would hate being assigned to a work detail that he secretly desires.

The conversation between an experienced convict and an employment officer might sound like this:

OFFICER: Okay, where do you want to work?

INMATE: I worked as a clerk in the library the last time I was here and I got burned. The job was too demanding and I couldn't get enough free time.

OFFICER: So are you saying you don't want a clerk's job?

INMATE: Yeah, I guess so. I don't think I could take working as a clerk anymore. I need something easier—you know, a no-brain job—so I can work on my legal papers and stuff like that.

OFFICER: So where do you want to be assigned?

INMATE: How about the kitchen? That's a pretty simple job and I get to eat real good. I think I'd like to work in the kitchen this time 'round. I got a couple of friends who work in the kitchen who can show me the ropes.

In this example, the inmate does his best to convince the employment officer that he really wants to be assigned to the kitchen detail, which is one of the worst jobs in any prison. The deception includes an explanation of why the inmate prefers this work detail even though the inmate knows that the prison official would consider this explanation as a reason *not* to assign him to the kitchen. (The inmate makes himself seem lazy. Also, having friends who already work in the kitchen suggests a possible conspiracy to smuggle food out.) According to the strategy behind playing the opposites, if the inmate manages to convince the employment officer that he really wants a job in the kitchen, he will be assigned a clerk's job, if one is available.

You would think that the risk of backfire would limit the use of playing the opposites, but, in fact, the game is popular among inmates. As for those who choose not to play, you can be certain they are careful not to let anyone know their real desires. Prisons seem to reward playing the opposites by punishing honesty.

When I first arrived at Graterford, I questioned the wisdom of this strategy. As a young man, I had been taught to "say what I mean, and mean what I say." More experienced inmates would often try to explain to me how that philosophy simply doesn't work in prison and that the best way for a prisoner to get what he wanted was to play the opposites. Thoughtful inmates told me that prison staff were trained not to care about inmates' personal preferences and were actually told to make prisoners as uncomfortable as possible. So when a prison administrator discovers an inmate's true preference, this knowledge will be used against him. Others simply said, "Who cares; all you need to know is that it works."

It was difficult for me to accept this conventional wisdom because I believed that corrections staff didn't have time to play petty mind games. I assumed that prison managers would treat inmates impartially. Impartial treatment would consider an individual's likes and dislikes when balanced with particular job availability and other situational factors. It made no sense to me that staff members would maliciously try to maximize the discomfort of inmates.

It was Clarence who convinced me there was more to playing the opposites than mere prison paranoia. Clarence was a drug dealer who was memorable for his razor-sharp wit and pungent sarcasm. One day, I found myself in a holding room seated next to him, as we waited to speak to the members of the Program Review Committee (PRC) to request a reduction in disciplinary sanctions for infractions we had committed. At the time, anyone who had received a disciplinary sanction could petition the PRC for a reduction of the punishment. The PRC required petitioning inmates to explain why they deserved a reduction in sanctions. Every Thursday, fifty or more inmates would be summoned to the holding room to make a plea for mercy before a panel of three high-ranking prison administrators who called themselves the PRC.

The disciplinary sanction I had received was cell restriction, so I was seated in the waiting room wearing my regular prison uniform. Clarence had been caught trying to smuggle drugs into the institution on a furlough return. Because he had received a disciplinary sanction of six months in the Hole, he was seated next to me in handcuffs, wearing standard dress for the Hole (a prison-stripes jumpsuit).

The PRC always took its time, so someone could expect to wait for hours to plead for mercy. The waiting room was small and unventilated, stuffed with many hot and sweaty men. Waiting in that room was extremely oppressive. I wondered if the PRC had intentionally designed the conditions in the room as a means to discourage men from seeking leniency. Several men left the waiting room in frustration, choosing to abandon their plans to address the PRC rather than to melt.

Clarence was prison-wise and determined to see the process through. He devised a plan to coax more of the men into leaving the room by complaining about the unpleasant conditions. He guessed this would shorten his waiting time.

"Watch this," he said to me, just before he spoke loudly to everyone in the room. "Man, these people must think we're real suckers. They got us all crowded in here sweating and smelling like plantation slaves waiting for their master to give them a neck bone or some other bullshit. Man, fuck the PRC."

This immediately caused some grumbling among the other men, and before long two or three of them left the waiting room. "That makes it a little bit easier to breathe in here," he whispered to me. No doubt, Clarence knew the angles, and that's why I was puzzled by his desire to see the PRC. Certainly, he didn't expect to get a reduction of his time in the Hole, considering the seriousness of his offense.

"What are you here for?" Clarence asked me.

"I'm on cell restriction for stupid stuff. My lock was broken and the guard couldn't unlock it with his key so he wrote me up," I explained.

"That's petty shit! That guard must not like you," he offered.

"I guess not. But tell me, do you really think the PRC is going to cut you any slack?" I asked.

"Sure, sure they will. I bet I get a break before you do!" he eagerly wagered.

"You've got to be kidding! I've got a meatball case and you're in the Hole for smuggling drugs and you think they'll give you a break? You'll be lucky if they don't give you a new street charge!" I scoffed in disbelief.

"Laugh if you want to. But I know how these people work and you don't. See, you'll probably go in there and tell them that you've been a good boy and that the guard was picking on you and that you'll never do it again. Man, they don't want to hear that shit! That's all they hear all day long. You better not tell them that sorry stuff," he warned.

"Yeah, well what do you plan on telling them?" I asked.

"I'm going to get on my hands and knees and beg them, I mean really beg them, to keep me in the damn Hole until they let me go home. That's what I'm going to do," he answered smartly.

"And that's your big plan? You think they'll feel sorry for you and just let you go? Why don't you ask for your drugs back while you're at it?" I asked sarcastically.

"Real funny. I can understand where you're coming from. You think these people care about you. You're really going to be shocked when you find out they don't give a shit about you or me. They couldn't care less about us waiting in this nasty room or you staying locked in your cell twenty-four hours a day because some guard has a hard-on for you. That's the bottom line. When you understand that, you'll stop doing hard time. See, I know they really want to put a foot up my ass, so when I go in there I'm going to let them do that. I'm going to tell those people that I was bringing the drugs in for a big, mean motherfucker in population and that if they let me out of the Hole, I'm going to get my ass kicked because I can't pay the dude back for the shit that was confiscated. I'm going to beg them not to let me out of the Hole. In fact, I'm going to ask for a transfer," he said with an impressive air of confidence.

"And that's your plan?" I asked.

"Yep, and if I were you, I'd figure out some reason to tell those people why you like it on cell restriction," he suggested.

We spoke together a little longer before the PRC finally escorted Clarence into the hearing room. About ten or fifteen minutes later I saw Clarence being taken back to the Hole. I remember thinking to myself that he was a fool to think that his scheme would work.

Eventually, the PRC called for me and I made my plea. As Clarence had predicted, I explained to the Committee that my infraction was a minor one. I noted that I had a history of good behavior and that I intended to obey all prison rules and regulations in the future. The PRC wasn't impressed and returned me to my cell to serve out the remainder of my restriction. I left the room angry, not for being turned down, but for having spent needless hours suffering in that hot and smelly holding room.

The next day, as I was reading in my cell, I heard a knock on the metal door. I looked up to see Clarence staring down at me. I couldn't believe it. The PRC had released him to the general population. His plan had worked!

"So I see you didn't take my advice," he said with a big grin. I was too stunned to respond. "Maybe this will teach you something about this place. These people don't care nothing about you and the sooner you realize that the better off you'll be." With that, he slowly walked away, whistling like a free man.

Not long after did I witness this lack of care in an old convict's story, a dark portrait of indignity and suffering that unfolded against the mean-spirited ethos of playing the opposites. He was oblivious to prison reality as he slowly, methodically swung his misshaped crutches forward to pull his broken body closer toward the dining hall. His distorted silhouette had shadowed the prison walkways for many years. He had come to a point in his life of captivity when the thought of freedom frightened him more than excited him.

With a hand-rolled "buckhorn" cigarette dangling from his lips, he mumbled, "Them eggs gonna be cold...I hate cold eggs. They're always cold." He complained to himself the way men do when they are more bored than angry.

No one listened to his protests because he was completely alone. His fellow convicts had long shunned him because he no longer had anything worth taking. The prison staff avoided him because they feared his misery might be contagious. As he hobbled along, the other inmates whizzed by him on their way to breakfast.

The rain forced the cripple to swing his body forward in very small, cautious advances. In the past, his heavy wood crutches had slipped on the wet concrete, causing him to fall and suffer great pain. A prison study once found that wooden, rubber-tipped crutches were better suited for prison use; their solid core made them too cumbersome to use as a weapon, and the absence of hollows prevented the stashing of contraband. But he was a simple man who knew only that these crutches were bulky and unwieldy, leaving him with callused hands and chafed underarms.

"Damn, these crutches," he cursed. "They're gonna make me miss breakfast." A cigarette ash dropped and disappeared into his damp, gray coat collar, becoming an insignificant part of an even more insignificant man.

People did not die of starvation in American prisons, and the old man knew it. But many did die of obscurity and that worried him. The only person concerned with his living or dying was the staff member who counted him during meals, and that was just to make sure that he did not exceed his allotted three meals a day.

Suddenly, his crutches slipped out from under him. He fell face down on the wet concrete walk and spit out his wet cigarette. "Shit, I can't miss chow," he said as he mustered his strength to rise.

The suspicious eye of a tower guard focused on his activity, watching him like a vulture, as the old man struggled on his way to the chow hall. "Inmate on the walk," the guard shouted, "keep moving. No loitering on the walk."

The old man ignored him but hurried on to avoid missing breakfast. "He knew I fell down. Why do they do things like that?" he asked no one in particular. "Don't they know by now I'm gonna get mine? Three hots and a cot is what they owe me, and that's what I'm gonna get."

Breathless and hungry, he finally reached the indoor entrance of the dining hall just in time to have another guard slam the barred gate in his face. The scent of cafeteria food invaded the old man's senses.

"The kitchen is closed, return to your block," ordered the guard.

"It was raining, and I fell. Slipped with these damn crutches," replied the old man, so angry that he began to cry. "Please let me eat," he begged, fighting back tears. "Just some coffee or a piece of bread. I'm an old man and I'm soaking wet. Please!"

The guard did not answer right away, staring back at him. "I can't let you," he said finally. "Breakfast is over, you know the rules."

"The game," the old man muttered to himself. "They insist on playing the game. But I'll beat them. I'll get my three hots." Then he said to the guard in a sad voice, "Yeah, those are the rules. Thanks anyway."

He turned his crippled body and slowly shuffled away. After making two swings of his crutches, he heard the guard call out to him, which brought a smile to the old man's face. He swung himself around to face the guard, knowing that his sympathy ploy had worked again.

"Look, Pop," said the guard, "you never caused me any trouble, so I'll tell you what I'm going to do. You go ahead over to see the kitchen steward. He's the one who can help you out. I'll give him a call and put in a good word for you."

"Thank you," said the old man. *The game, they gotta play the game. He could have let me in,* he thought as he swung around in the direction of the kitchen steward's office.

"Watch the waxed floor, Pop," cautioned the guard. "We wouldn't want you to fall and hurt yourself."

The steward's office was located down a long, concrete corridor that had just been waxed, leaving a gray, treacherous film that even right-walking men slipped on. In the past, the old man never even knew it was there until he finally fell several times. In fact, it was the cumulative effects of all those occasional falls that had crippled his legs, bent his back, and broken his spirit.

"The damn game, the damn slippery floor, these damn crutches," he cursed in cadence with each swing of his crutches.

Surprisingly, he reached the steward's office without falling. A man sat at a desk, while inmate workers pushed large carts of cooked food back and forth through the kitchen.

"What do you need?" asked the desk man without looking up.

"The kitchen guard sent me. I missed breakfast."

"Yeah, he called a while ago. Sounds like you've been through a lot. You must be hungry."

"Yes, I am."

"You hurt? Need to go to the infirmary or something?"

"No, sir. I just need to eat, that's all."

"Yeah, I bet you do." There was a brief silence. "I'm going to have to get the steward. He's the man to see." The desk man rose and left the office.

"More games," mumbled the old man. "He should have told me he wasn't the steward."

Finally, a short, fat steward entered, still chewing his breakfast. "You missed breakfast?"

"Yes, sir, I did."

"The officer called and told me all about it."

"I've never been late before."

"No, you haven't. I would have recognized you. Look, I have no problem feeding you. God knows I have more than enough food. But first, you have to get permission from the major of the guards. He has the final say in these matters. I'll call and tell him you're coming. And," the steward added conspiratorially, "I'll tell him it's okay with me."

"Thank you, sir."

"No problem. You know where the major's office is?"

"Yes, sir, I do."

Another disappointment on this particularly trying day. Like a rat chasing a piece of cheese, the old cripple negotiated the long, slippery maze and ventured up two full flights of stairs. After a long ordeal, he eventually arrived at the major's office to find yet another desk man.

"Are you the major?"

"No," the desk clerk answered. "What is it you want?"

"I'm here to see the major."

"I kind of figured that. Now tell me why."

The old convict reluctantly recounted his tale, wondering if they all enjoyed hearing these bad-luck stories.

"You must be the one the steward called about," said the desk man. "The major's reading your file now. He's been expecting you." With that, he abruptly left the room.

The old man waited in silence, knowing that it was all part of the game to see how high he would jump or how low he would go. But he could not understand why he let himself be the main attraction in this dog-and-pony show.

The major finally arrived, a cup of coffee and an unfinished danish in his hands. He tossed both into a waste can close to the old man. The aroma of trashed coffee and pastry wafted its way up to the inmate's nose.

"I want you to know I'm a very busy man," said the major. "I don't really have the time to deal with matters like this. However, because the kitchen steward called me, I did read your file."

"Yes, sir, major, you can see I never did this before."

"Yes, I noticed that. It also tells me you never got caught before. You must be a very smooth operator."

The gambit had been played. The major was trying to provoke him.

"Sir, all I want is something to eat," countered the old man. "I really couldn't help falling."

"I'm sure you couldn't, and if it were up to me, I would certainly make sure you got your meal. It is bad policy to deny an inmate his food. Makes us appear cruel. But administrative directives require the warden to make such decisions."

The old man sighed. "I was only a few minutes late. That's all. These damn crutches, they're just no good in the rain."

"Don't blame your irresponsibility on your crutches. It always seems to be someone else's fault, never yours. Well, save your story for the warden. He'll want to know why you missed breakfast. Okay, you can go now."

The major disappeared from the room.

"All I want is a meal," mumbled the inmate, as he laboriously swung his crutches toward the warden's office. He endured yet another maze and two more upward flights of stairs, his mutterings echoing off the masonry walls.

"So it's come to this. They got me begging for a free meal. I've robbed, stolen, and done a lot of lousy things, but I never made a hungry man beg for food. And they wonder why I hate them. They're the real criminals."

At long last, he entered the warden's spacious, well-furnished office. A large basket of fruit caught his eye, within arm's reach, mocking his hunger.

"May I help you?" asked a secretary behind the fruit.

"The major sent me to talk to the warden."

"We've been expecting you. The warden will be with you in a moment."

Another long silence ensued, as the inmate tried not to think about his hunger or his misery. No matter what the Warden said, he knew that he would have to travel back down four flights of stairs, any victory ultimately his loss.

A deep voice startled him out of his reverie. "So, you're the man who missed his breakfast," said the warden, the convict's file in his hand.

"Yes, I am."

"I've reviewed your file. Despite your disability, there is no reason for you not to get to your meals on time. You've been issued crutches to accommodate your condition." He paused to study the old man's appearance. "The major of the guard tells me you claim to have fallen on your way to breakfast. Something about your crutches slipping on the wet concrete. Is that correct?"

"Yes, sir."

"Well, you know that is impossible. Those crutches are specially designed to resist slipping on wet surfaces. If you really did fall, it can only be because you were negligent in their use. Do you agree with that?"

During a moment that seemed a lifetime, the old man was forced to decide whether a meal was worth the humiliation of admitting to a wrong he had not committed. All he wanted was a meal. But if he did not agree with the warden, he knew he would not get his meal. If he did agree, he knew he would also be eating his own pride.

"Yes, sir," he said without hesitation.

"Good, good. I'm going to approve your request for a late breakfast. But rest assured, I will be closely monitoring your conduct in the future. I will not tolerate carelessness or lateness. You will eat with all the other inmates. Do you understand?"

"Yes, sir."

"Very good. You report to the steward's office. He'll give you a late pass to the dining hall."

The long, hazardous descent down four flights of stairs afforded the old man time to reflect on the events that had just transpired. He asked himself, "Why did I humiliate myself for that meal? They'll serve lunch in a few hours. I wouldn't have starved. Why did I do that?"

Suddenly, his crutches slipped and sent him tumbling down the final flight of stairs. He lay face down on the stairway, his crutches several feet below, knowing he would have to crawl down to get to his crutches and then to his pass. Then it struck him why he had agreed with the warden, who he was, and what he had become. He decided not to move. Not to eat. His needs didn't count.

These weren't the only incidents in my prison experience to convince me that there is merit to playing the opposites, but they certainly were among the most memorable. I've personally chosen not to play the game; when it comes to expressing my real preferences in prison, I generally remain silent. Still, because I recognize that playing the opposites is an effective tool for getting what you want from prison staff, I've advised inexperienced inmates of its benefits.

If it were simply a "prison thing," playing the opposites wouldn't be of much importance, other than reinforcing stereotypes of inmates as manipulative and dishonest. But the truth is that playing the opposites is an age-old strategy employed by all oppressed people.

I realized this after reading a collection of Uncle Remus stories, tales that were passed down orally by generations of black slaves in America. In one story, Br'er Fox (symbolizing the master) was trying to catch Br'er Rabbit (symbolizing the slave). Br'er Fox fashioned a trap for the rabbit by making a tarbaby (a doll covered with sticky tar) and leaving it out in a field. Br'er Rabbit, thinking the tarbaby was another animal, walked over to talk to it. Gradually, he became ensnared, hopelessly stuck to the doll. The gleeful fox ran out of hiding, gloating about the different ways he might choose to kill the rabbit. Playing along, Br'er Rabbit begged not to be thrown into a nearby brier-patch because, he explained, it would be unbearable to be torn to pieces in the thorns. Naturally, the malicious fox immediately tossed him into the briers. Waiting in the patch were Br'er Rabbit's friends, who freed him from the tarbaby. Hopping away, the clever rabbit ridiculed the fox for being so gullible.

This story reminded me of Clarence in the PRC waiting room. Apparently, playing the opposites is not only an adjustment to prison life but also a survival tactic of the disadvantaged everywhere. It is a practice employed by all rabbits, slaves, and inmates to defend themselves against all foxes, masters, and prison staff. The most troubling aspect of this adjustment is that it encourages deceit as an acceptable means to an end and, in the old man's case, punishes honesty. In prison, it is hard to know when an inmate is being truthful or when he is playing the opposites. The longer a person remains in prison, the less likely it is that he will be able to share sincere feelings with anyone, a penalty of the ground rules of this game.

Staff are not exempt from the far-reaching effects of these lies. Some officials don't believe anything an inmate says, or they believe the opposite of whatever inmates tell them. In response, some inmates intentionally tell the truth in situations where they know they won't be trusted, perpetuating a cycle of deceit that makes communication almost impossible in prison.

So go the frustrating conversations between foxes and rabbits everywhere, trading an ounce of comic relief in the brier-patch for a pound of distrust, cynicism, and despair in the fields.

7

The Politics of Persecution

I have always considered myself a proud American and, despite my incarceration, I still subscribe to the traditional American system of values. Before coming to prison, I expected it to be a very unpleasant place, staffed by the otherwise unemployable and inhabited by the generally unredeemable. While I was not surprised by the amount of violence and corruption at Graterford, I was genuinely shocked by the level of persecution.

One illustration of the politics of anger was revealed to me soon after my ill-fated hamburger caper. There was an unexpected consequence to that infraction of which I was not initially aware. After my misconduct hearing, I returned to my cell to begin serving my sixty days of cell restriction. At the time, I genuinely felt I was being mistreated. Compared with the rampant thievery and abundance of violence I had witnessed in Graterford, my measly infraction was hardly worth the bother. Losing my job and paying for the burgers made sense, but two months locked in my cell for twenty-two hours a day seemed unfair to me.

Little did I realize that there were higher forces who felt I had been treated too leniently and who wanted to thrust me into the lions' den of jailhouse politics. In actual fact, stealing food from a penitentiary kitchen was a serious offense because it involved two vital concerns of the administration: spending and control. Graterford spent an average of $2.75 per day to feed a single inmate, in contrast to the statewide average of about $2.10 per day. To the powers that be, the ease with which I was able to buy smuggled food from the kitchen meant that the prison could not control its inmates. If other inmates similarly challenged its control, the per diem cost of feeding the population could rise drastically.

Ten pounds of bootlegged ground beef should have landed me directly in the Hole. The fact that I used the major of the guards' bathroom in my plot normally should also have cost me double time in cold storage for my arrogant defiance of authority. If anything, cell restriction was a lucky break for me. But what did I know? I hadn't been in prison long enough to appreciate the seriousness of the situation.

When I finally arrived at my cell, I was unexpectedly greeted by the B-Block sergeant. A man of military bearing, he stood a rigid six feet tall in a starched and precisely creased uniform. His prison dress cap added height to his authority.

"Didn't think I'd be seeing you back so soon," the sergeant said, chewing on a lump of tobacco in his cheek that gave his southern drawl a lazier tone. He spat to accentuate his words. I assumed he was referring to my returning so soon from the misconduct hearing. Usually men given cell restriction took their time coming back in an effort to extend their liberties.

"I got sixty days cell restriction, Sarge," I complained naively. "Can you believe that?"

The sergeant spat again. "Boy, the way I see it, you must be a real important inmate to have talked your way out of the Hole. I don't like important inmates on my block, so you just watch yourself because you can be right sure I'll be watching you."

With that, he double-locked me in and walked away like a general who had just reviewed his troops. Amazed by his hostility, I foolishly thought he was singling me out for some personal reason, perhaps because I was Jewish.

However, the truth was that the sergeant's attitude had nothing to do with me but with my former work supervisor, the major of the guard, who had intervened on my behalf to keep me out of the Hole. This recently appointed officer happened to be the only African American in Pennsylvania history to hold such a position. As such, he was the first member of a minority to personally direct the actions of a historically all-white guard force at Graterford. In addition he had been promoted from the rank of lieutenant, which was not only unprecedented but also caused a stir among the several captains he was promoted over.

To further complicate the situation, the major was also a reformer, a compassionate and decent man who did not feel that physical force was the way to solve Graterford's problems. In his view, such a traditional style of prison management often led to the unfair treatment that had thrust Graterford into a crisis in the first place.

While the prison administration and the overwhelmingly African American inmate population were hopeful about the major, the almost all-white, rank-and-file staff were disgruntled over his appointment. Not only had a longstanding race barrier been broken, but also there was genuine concern that the major's management style would give the prison away to the inmates. Militarism and white leadership had been the way at Graterford for generations.

When the major had decided that my actions were not serious enough to warrant sending me to the Hole, battle lines were drawn. Derogatory slurs were already being made about him by the uniformed staff, often in the presence of inmates, which only served to undermine the major's authority.

There I was in the middle of all this, and I didn't even know it. I simply wasn't yet tuned in to the political undercurrents sweeping through Graterford.

While on cell restriction, I was let out of my cell for two hours each day for recreation. During this time, I found myself and my cell constantly being searched by the block guards. Although they were not as intrusive as they could have been, even one search of a man's cell or body is an assault on his sense of dignity and freedom.

Naturally, my resentment and paranoia grew with each search, as if every guard was out to get me. Helpless to stop them, I began to hate these men in uniform. To make matters worse, some of them would ridicule and taunt me by calling me the "major's boy." At times they would even imply that I had avoided the Hole by being a snitch. The mere suggestion of such a label in a prison like Graterford was life threatening.

On the fifty-ninth day of my sixty days of cell restriction, I was issued another misconduct—for taking more than two hours for recreation. Reporting to another misconduct hearing, I was given an additional thirty days of cell restriction. As I returned to my cell, the sergeant was again waiting for me.

He spat a wad. "Boy, I don't know why you came back to this block. You got no job and you just keep breaking the rules." He spat again. "You must know some real important people. But let me tell you this. Let any of my officers catch you wrong again and nobody's going to be able to save you then."

This time I said nothing, although I'm certain the hatred beating in my heart could be heard by the sergeant as he locked me in and paraded out of sight. For all my frustration and anger, I was too young and inexperienced to realize that his malice was focused elsewhere. The old soldier was just trying to stop the process of change. His real enemy was the black major with his liberal notions. I was just someone who was unlucky enough to be chosen as the vehicle for his resentment.

Resistance to change in a prison can foment enough resentment and malice to result in changes so riddled with compromise that more problems are created than solved. The only beneficiaries of this kind of change are those who will profit from the system's breakdown. As a twenty-two-year veteran of jailhouse politics, I can now only speculate what could have transpired had the sergeant approved of the major. Could Graterford have become a better place? No one will ever know.

The sergeant did much to shape my current reality. He accomplished this by continuing to have the block guards pat me down and search my cell, even after I had completed all my cell-restriction time. Generally, this type of treatment was reserved for troublemakers and drug dealers. I was neither. Although the searches never turned up anything of consequence, my cell was always left in total disarray. My creature comforts, such as an extra pillow, bed sheet, and towel, were taken away from me.

Beyond the unfair treatment, the sergeant had succeeded in making me feel even more isolated from the world that existed outside the prison walls. I was no longer so proud to be an American. I was just a convict without rights. Again, I had simply misconstrued the motives behind his actions.

When prison guards feel they are losing control, their first response is to crack down hardest on the segment of the population over whom they still have control. This is done as a show of force to let the general population know that they mean business. Furthermore, if cooperative inmates are being treated this harshly, then the troublesome ones can expect much more serious treatment.

The problem with this control tactic is that it doesn't always work. Often the uncooperative elements of the population don't necessarily get the message or don't care about the consequences of their actions. When this happens, conditions usually worsen. There is still a control problem, only now it exists with the added hostility and resentment of the more stable inmates.

I was now made to feel the full weight of forced confinement in an imposed egalitarian police state. All my life I had been taught to work for my livelihood; the harder I worked and the more resourceful I was, the greater would be my reward. Now everything was turned around. No matter how hard I worked, or even if I worked at all, I received the same portion as everyone else. There was no incentive to achieve anything or improve myself. In fact, the more well-behaved I was, the more likely it was that I would be mistreated by inmates and staff.

Anger affects every aspect of prison life and management. At Graterford it made victims of the major, the sergeant, and me. We were all left wondering what kind of world we had fashioned and, each in our own way, resented having to live in it. While anger usually demands satisfaction, it often settles just for company. I had now resolved that the inmate population would be my new nation. And the first thing I would do was join the Graterford Lifers Organization.

"I need a pass for the Lifers meeting," I told the guard seated at a small, shabby desk in the middle of the B-Block "Bridge." The Bridge was a ten-foot walkway that spanned the two upper-tier walkways of the block like the center crossline of a big "H." Behind me stood twenty other men waiting for their passes off the block. I spent a good deal of my time at Graterford waiting in one line or another.

"I didn't know you were a lifer," replied the weary, disaffected bridge officer, a phone receiver cradled between his shoulder and ear. Routine had just about made him a part of the furniture he was stuck in. His hands quickly fingered my inmate ID card, but he never looked up. He knew me only from the identity photo.

Without answering, I silently waited for my pass. He slid back to me a standardized slip of paper and my ID card. I took both immediately and headed down to the ground floor of B-Block.

Once I reached the block's main entrance, I waited my turn in yet another line, this time for the front-door officer to allow me off the block.

"I didn't know you were a lifer," the door guard said, echoing the bridge officer.

Again I waited silently until he decided to verify my pass. I then entered the main corridor and merged with a moving mass of inmates. During general movement, hundreds of men walked quickly up and down the corridor. Most of them wore prison uniforms for work or exercise clothes for the yard, but there were always some in pajamas and bathrobes whose only apparent purpose was to be part of the confusion.

As I headed for the auditorium, I could hear the familiar voices of hustlers hawking sandwiches, drugs, and anything else worth selling. Hundreds of voices bounced off the concrete walls, the usual disconcerting din that always heightened my concern that I might accidentally collide with the wrong guy. Sometimes the carnival atmosphere here made me forget the dangers of this place. But invariably, I would witness the all too common corridor knifing and be reminded once again how risky it was to commute on this prison's main boulevard.

Halfway to E-Block, I arrived at the main entrance of the auditorium, one of its four doors wedged open with a guard blocking the way inside. I gave him my pass, which he glanced at and quickly returned without a word. All his attention was focused on the many shadows speeding past him in both directions. There were no other guards in sight, so his safety was more of a priority than my status as a lifer. Besides, who would attend a Lifers meeting if he wasn't a lifer?

Crumpling the pass and tossing it, I stepped inside into a dusky twilight. The auditorium, used on weekends as a movie theater, had its lights dimmed down to ambush dark. This would explain why the door guard chose to take his chances in the more brightly lit corridor.

A few feet inside, I was greeted by the first row of steel-framed theater chairs. The auditorium could seat about a thousand men in three descending columns of these battered folding seats. Deep within was a flat area of space flanked by two basketball hoops mounted on the wall. Directly adjacent to this was an elevated stage that stood a few feet off the floor. It had a large, dirty white projection screen pulled down in front of it.

As I looked down at the farthest row of seats, I could see about a hundred indistinguishable figures standing, sitting, or slouching. Three men stood alone together, facing the audience.

I couldn't make out anybody I knew well enough to sit next to, so I just walked down to the third row and took an aisle seat. Soon after, I heard the sound of a heavy steel door slam and lock. Shut in from the noisy corridor, I was unaccustomed to such eerie quiet.

"I call this meeting to order," said the tallest of the three standing men.

I had never been to a Lifers meeting and I wasn't sure I wanted to be there now to listen to some of Pennsylvania's most vicious killers. But since I'd become one of the boys, I decided it was time to meet my fellow lifers. Besides, I longed to be a part of a self-governing body.

There were three inmate social organizations in Graterford at the time: the Lifers Organization, the Knights of Henry Christof, and the Jaycees (Junior Chamber of Commerce). Each of them was allowed to raise funds in the prison through the sale of food or by providing services, such as showing movies and taking photos in the visiting room. Prison gangs would inevitably dominate these groups and try to control or manipulate any money-making ventures that they undertook.

As the tall man spoke, everyone appeared attentive. The meeting followed a reasonable order of business, with questions asked and politely answered. I soon felt so completely at ease that I wanted to join the discussion in some way.

The tall man gave the floor to the shortest man, apparently the financial officer, who started giving a business report. I knew the Lifers sold soda and potato chips to the population on weekends during the auditorium movies. What I didn't know was that they were allowed to make profits and maintain a bank account. I was thrilled to hear that a private enterprise zone actually existed in Graterford. Maybe a little too thrilled.

When the speaker concluded his report, I enthusiastically stood up and asked a question. "Excuse me, I heard you say we have money in a bank account. I just wondered, how much do we have on deposit and how much revenue do we generate?"

I don't know why I stood up but, from the sudden focus of attention on me and the mumbling around me, I realized that standing up in a Lifers meeting meant a lot more than I had intended. Things got ugly real quick.

"Why do you want to know?" asked the speaker.

"Well, I just wondered how much money we were making," I replied a little defensively.

"What are you, a troublemaker?"

"What are you talking about? I asked a simple question and I'd like an answer." Instinct had trained me not to let anyone talk down to me.

It was obvious I had hit a nerve. The prudent thing would have been to sit down quietly and forget the whole matter. But prudence in Graterford was seldom a viable option because it was often mistaken for weakness.

"Why don't you sit down and dig yourself," said the tall speaker.

At this point I felt a tugging at my shirt sleeve. An older man in his mid-forties materialized in the seat beside mine, smiling up at me. As my focus was on the escalating trouble in front of me, I just pulled my arm away and answered the speaker.

"I'll sit down when I get an answer."

The tall man took a step toward me, and I turned toward the aisle to confront him. Once again I felt that tugging at my sleeve and glanced over at the widening smile of my neighbor.

The short speaker reclaimed my attention. "Look, why don't you just sit down."

Someone behind me called out, "Sit the fuck down, motherfucker!"

Then someone else shouted, "Answer the man's question!"

Things were obviously getting out of control, as my fellow lifers now tried to egg on a confrontation. Painfully, I knew I would have to remain standing until I got an answer, no matter what happened.

The third man, who had said nothing so far, finally broke his silence. "Look, all of this noise is going to get the guards into our business." Then he addressed me, "Now look, I ain't never seen you at a meeting before. I don't even know if you're really a lifer. Besides, we ain't got this month's statement yet."

The three then began to speak among themselves. The tallest one had to be pulled back from advancing toward me.

Before I got a chance to decide what to do, I was pulled down into my seat by the smiling man. He never gave me a chance to speak.

"You are either the bravest man I have ever met or the dumbest. It's too early to tell which." This wasn't said offensively, and the man's demeanor was so kindly that I had to appreciate his sense of humor. But I still kept one eye on the three speakers.

"Now just sit where you're at and try not to say anything," he continued. "You made your point. What you need to do now is take a look behind you and see what you got started. Those three guys up there are really not your major problem."

Cautiously I glanced back. I was surprised to see how many men were standing up and looking in our direction. There was a lot of cursing, mumbling, and even a few snarls. I turned back around.

"What are they all so mad about?"

"Mad?" The smiling man belly laughed. "They're not mad. They're just warming up."

Almost on cue, one of the men directly behind us stood up and hollered, "You know I'm a lifer, motherfucker, now you tell me about that money. And don't give me no shit about you don't know. You ain't pulling that on me. This ain't my first time here."

Someone else shouted out, "Man, don't be feeding into that negative shit. Sit the fuck down!"

Yet another voice called out, "Man, fuck that! What's wrong with knowing how much money we got?"

The guy directly behind me answered, "They stealing, that's what's wrong."

"So who ain't?" shouted a faraway voice.

A dozen men were now arguing among themselves, some holding others back. It looked like a fight was about to break out at any minute. Nevertheless, my companion just continued to smile as he shook his head.

"It sure doesn't take much to get these men started," he said.

Still a little confused about what was going on, I just looked at him in silent amazement.

"Let me ask you a question," he said. "Did you happen to notice that the guard locked us all in here with no supervision? Do you know why he did that?"

I shook my head.

"Because he knows that everybody in this room has at least one confirmed homicide to his credit. And obviously being smarter than us both, he decided he didn't want to be caught in a dark room alone with a bunch of murderers who might start fighting. Now tell me, what do you suggest we do if things turn ugly?"

His words left me speechless.

"I thought so. You haven't got a plan. You're just playing out of pocket. Well then, you might as well tell me your name so, if I get my old behind in a tussle, I'll know who to thank."

It took me a moment to answer. "My name's Victor, but I really didn't mean..."

"It's too late to sweat it now. I just hope you can fight as good as you can talk, because you managed to embarrass some of the men in here."

"But all I did was ask a question."

"That's all it takes in this place. People don't like to answer a whole lot of questions, especially about money, especially if they're stealing. I'd be surprised if they weren't. By the way, my name is Harold, but I prefer to be called Omar. I don't like being called by my slave name." With that he extended his hand to me.

I gladly shook Omar's hand. It looked like I might be needing a friend. Besides, there was something about him that I really liked and admired. Nothing seemed to rattle him.

To our relief, things were settling down. Almost everybody was sitting down now, although with a cautious edge.

"Why does everyone seem so angry all the time?" I asked my new friend.

"Good question. It's probably because most of the men in here take everything personally. Nothing's really personal unless you want it to be. Or it could be that anger is really all the authorities leave you that's your own. They take everything else away from you at Receiving. Now, why don't we start easing toward the door so that, when the guard decides to open up, we can slip out of here without getting our feelings hurt."

With that sage advice, Omar and I got up and walked up the aisle. He was smiling and chuckling, which took some of the tension out of the air, occasionally calling out or waving to one of his friends.

Once we made it to the auditorium door, Omar turned to me and said, "Victor, you live a charmed life. You may even manage to come out of this with a little rep [reputation]. In the future, try not to upset anybody and always make sure you have a way out before you start asking questions. Frankly, you like things a little too exciting for me."

In time, Omar and I became as close as brothers. The population would come to know us collectively as the Muslim and the Jew. And it was through Omar's wisdom that I learned that nothing in prison is personal.

Not long after my first Lifers meeting, Omar became my closest friend and my window into the workings of prison life. He knew many of the inmates at Graterford and understood better than I the language, games, players, and dangers of the prison system. Most important, he was willing to share his wisdom with me. His profound insight into the system helped me to grope my way through a foreign country of which I had had no inkling before I arrived at Graterford. Thus, Omar became my Old Head and I became his eager disciple.

A few months after I had lost my job in the major's office, Omar was hired to take my place. Because he now lived on the same block as I did, I often visited him in his cell. We ate meals together, walked the yard together, and exchanged a lot of jailhouse philosophy to kill time. We became inseparable and were one of the more unusual sights in Graterford: the veteran black Muslim from Philadelphia and the young Jewish rookie from New Jersey. We were constantly arguing about one issue or another.

I would often find my Old Head sitting on the cold, hard concrete floor of his cell, deeply absorbed in writing a letter to his family but never turning his back to the doorway, always keeping one cautious eye on the inmate traffic a few feet away. His cell was drab and spartan, containing little more than state-issued clothing, bedding, and some old newspapers. I once asked Omar why he chose to have so few possessions.

"I don't like people taking things away from me," he replied. "If I don't have anything in here that's mine, then the authorities can't take away any more than they already have. Besides, I don't think it's healthy for a man to get too comfortable in the slammer."

On one occasion I had just returned from a prison basketball game that had ended in a vicious melee between a black and a white gang. Often one prison gang would field a team to play against a team backed by another gang, and the rivalry on the court usually led to violence. Watching who won the game was only half as exciting as watching who won the fight *after* the game.

But today I was particularly disturbed by the rampant hatred and racism between black and white inmates, so I posed a naive question to Omar: "Why do they hate and hurt each other so much? Why don't they just get together and channel their hatred toward the guards?"

Omar's ubiquitous grin vanished. After a long stare that was pregnant with pause, he finally said: "It's all a game."

"What, that's it?" I protested. "All the beatings, stabbings, and killings are just a game? It's no game. Men dying is no game."

Omar regarded me with some amazement. I must have been a bit more excited than I had intended. With a gentle but serious tone he cautioned, "Are you going to argue with me or are you going to listen?"

I sat quietly, waiting for him to share his view of the restless shadow world we lived in. Just outside his cell, silent, unfriendly faces glided past, glancing inside, never smiling. It was this kind of backdrop that kept a man alert in his cell at all times. Occasionally a prison guard would look in on us and then move on. Although I was not allowed to enter another man's cell, the rule was never enforced.

"Most of the hate and anger in here is all a game," Omar emphasized again. "It's a hustle, just another way for people to make money. Anger and hatred are a prison's cash crop.

"When whites hate blacks, they're stealing the sympathy and favor of a mostly white Christian administration. When blacks hate whites, they're strong-arming appeasements and concessions. The administration, they get the most out of it all. Violence and hatred in prison means more money, more guards, more overtime, and more prisons. What incentive is there to keep prisons safe and humane? All staff has to do is sit back and let the men here tear each other apart. Then they can cry to the legislatures and tell them how much more money they need to control their prison. Just like with the prison swag men, dope boys, and laundry men, there's something being sold and money being made. Only it's a lot more money than most of the guys in here can ever imagine. It's a lot easier for everyone to profit from hatred than it is to help the poor and ignorant do something positive with their lives."

I couldn't believe what I was hearing. "Come on, Omar, you can't believe that stuff. You're sounding real paranoid, like there's a conspiracy everywhere." His views were similar to those of others, who believed the administration was actually encouraging gang activity. But I wasn't ready to believe either one of them. The prison system was too chaotic to be that deliberate.

Omar replied, "Well, then you tell me why, with all the guards, guns, locks, gates, walls, and money, they still can't stop what's going on in here?"

I had no answer to that. "Okay, if this is all a game and everybody knows it, then why do the men in here play it? Why do they play when it can get them hurt and even killed?"

Omar smiled assuredly. "It's like a Dodge City crap game in here, Victor. Everyone who plays it knows it's crooked, but they play it anyway—because it's the only game in town."

8

Society of Captives

By the mid-1980s, Graterford was in the advanced stages of a complete system breakdown. Not only had the prison become an extremely violent place, but also the administration was showing signs of an inability to meet the inmate population's basic need for food and shelter. This breakdown, however, opened the door for a thriving underground economy that provided virtually every kind of goods and services that the legitimate prison system now lacked.

One service was drugs. Drug dealers in prison often use homosexuals to smuggle contraband. For this reason, some homosexuals in prison enlarge their anal cavities so they can hide drugs in greater quantities. Since many prison "mules" work on a percentage basis, larger cavities translate into more money. Mules are sometimes even paid to carry contraband in their cavities all day long. They become walking safe-deposit boxes. Dealers get rich because there is a strong demand for drugs to help people get through the day.

Other services were more like standard amenities. For example, if I wanted my laundry done, I could pay an inmate laundry worker with cigarettes to have my laundry picked up, cleaned, and delivered back to me. If, on the other hand, I had tried to send my laundry through the institution's authorized laundry system, I probably would never have gotten it back. Thieves and hustlers who profited from the underground laundry made sure that the prison laundry was unable to meet the population's needs. So for two or three fifty-cent packs a week, an inmate could get his laundry cleaned and returned, which was a real bargain. Those who had no cigarettes wore dirty clothes or washed their own laundry.

Other black-market services abounded at Graterford, especially in the main corridor where most business was conducted. For a few packs a week, a swag man could deliver specialized cooked foods and pastries to your cell on a daily basis. The food was smuggled out of the kitchen by inmate workers who would then openly hawk them on any housing block. These swag men were the most prolific of the underground service providers and, because the food cost them nothing, also the best paid. The quality of bootlegged sandwiches was comparable to or better than that of the food served in the dining hall. But this said more about the breakdown of Graterford's food service than about the culinary skills of the swag men.

Eventually, I worked my way into a situation where my own basic needs were being met. I had at my disposal the eager services of swag men, laundry men, ice men (for summer ice cubes), barbers (to cut my hair in my cell), and phone men (to make sure I was signed up for phone calls). I could even have a cell cleaner, although I felt there were certain things a man should do for himself. All in all, Graterford had become a predatory institution where nothing worked right and everything was for sale. Most of the violence was now directed at people who failed to pay their debts. The underground economy was so healthy at this point that it needed to take further steps to defend and preserve its fiscal survival.

Graterford the prison became Graterford the ghetto: A place where men forgot about courts of law or the differences between right and wrong because they were too busy thinking about living, dying, or worse. Reform, rehabilitation, and redemption do not exist in a ghetto. There is only survival of the fittest.

Crime, punishment, and accountability are of little significance when men are living in a lawless society where their actions are restrained only by the presence of concrete and steel. Where a prison in any real or abstract sense might promote the greater good, once it becomes a ghetto it can do nothing but promise violent upheaval. As weapons in Graterford proliferated, violence escalated, and gang leadership emerged; the administration gradually ceded control of the institution to independent gang tribes.

Generally, black gangs in Graterford were extensions of Philadelphia's neighborhood street gangs. They bore names based on their urban location, for example, the 21st and Norris Gang, the 60th and Market Gang, the 10th Street Gang, and so forth. Many of their members had belonged to the original street gang before they were incarcerated. Once sent to Graterford, they joined their prison counterpart to carry on the gang's traditions. As more and more street-gang members arrived, their growing strength in numbers enabled them to conduct a wider array of prison-gang activities.

The moment any African American Philadelphian entered the prison, scouts immediately approached him to determine which part of the city he came from and whether he had been a member of a street gang. This sorting of incoming blacks based on geography dictated the character of black prison gangs, giving rise to the often-used term "homey" for those who hailed from the same neighborhood or hometown. Homeys were the most common recruits for black-gang membership.

Black gangs competed vigorously with each other for turf and the control of contraband sales. While this competition often resulted in violent battles, gangs on many occasions merged their enterprises and worked together. For example, rival gangs had been known to fight each other over the business of selling drugs, yet they frequently cooperated in bringing the drugs into the prison.

Those black gangs formed by inmates from areas other than Philadelphia differed considerably from the black Philly gangs in that, for the most part, they had no counterparts on the streets. Such non-Philly gangs usually originated in the prison and their members were often strangers who happened to be from the same county or city. The competition between regional gangs and Philly gangs tended to be very hostile and violent. There was seldom any trust or cooperation between them. Numerically, Philly gangs greatly outnumbered other gangs, which allowed them to dominate the population and completely exclude outsiders from joint ventures.

Regardless of their numerical superiority, it is highly probable that Philly gangs still would have had more control, because their carry-over from street gangs gave them the distinct advantage of functioning under well-established rules, organizational structures, leadership systems, and ideologies. In contrast, regional or prison-based gangs tended to be weakened internally by frequent power struggles, uncertain leadership, and untested organizational processes.

Because Graterford's black gangs were determined almost exclusively by geography, gang membership was widely diverse. In any one gang you could expect to find drug addicts, thieves, murderers, and hustlers of every stripe, including Muslims, Christians, and atheists.

This amalgam of homeys provided black-gang members with such strength and vitality that the administration was hard pressed to break them apart.

Black gangs at Graterford primarily operated as money-making enterprises. While geography helped to bring prison gang members together, it was money and drugs that kept them together. The goal of every gang was to earn money, which meant selling anything that anyone was willing to buy. As in a corporation, gang profits were then reinvested to buy more contraband for further distribution. Gang members gauged their individual value by the amount of money they were able to make. What they did with their earnings was of no consequence, because the hustle itself seemed to be all that mattered. Money earned was merely an indicator of how good a hustler an inmate could be.

White gangs at Graterford were a completely different story. These gangs almost always originated in prison and, like the non-Philly gangs, were not as well-structured or established. They too were composed of members who were often strangers to each other, most of them brought together by the simple chance of their skin color.

Statistically, white gangs in Graterford were strictly a minority, usually formed for their own protection from other gangs. While they might be involved in some hustling, they were limited by their inability to protect their turf or business interests against the larger black gangs. They were more likely to be the buyers of drugs and contraband than the sellers.

Furthermore, most white gang members were not brought together by geography but rather out of a need to protect their mutual interests. White drug addicts tended to join together to pool their funds to buy drugs at a volume discount. Some white gangs were formed because of ethnic bonds, such as Catholics, Italians, and Protestants, or because of special interests, such as gamblers and bodybuilders.

White gangs at Graterford were more likely to be small, improvised groups rather than organized teams with specific agendas, and were generally much less diverse than their black counterparts. Whereas black gangs required large memberships to generate income and protect their turf, white gangs preferred to have as few members as possible in an effort to stretch their resources. Any white gang that grew too large would promptly be challenged by the dominant black gangs.

The exceptions in Graterford were the outlaw motorcycle gangs that successfully managed to entrench themselves within the prison system. Like the Hell's Angels who had already established themselves on the street, they were far more business oriented and could compete directly with black gangs in the sale of contraband, drugs in particular. Despite their relatively small numbers in the prison, their connections to the much larger street gangs made them resourceful money makers and a power to be reckoned with.

By 1984, Graterford's population exceeded 2500. Gangs proliferated at a staggering rate, not only because of high unemployment inside the prison but also because of the need for protection from the gangs' new money-making schemes. If you couldn't rob a man's cell, you just robbed the man himself. On occasion you snatched an exposed wallet from a careless guard's pants or jacket pocket. Anyone and anything was fair game. Extortion became very lucrative. One of the favorite ways to deal with a resistant victim was to lock him in his cell and set the cell on fire. So if you were not aligned with a protection gang soon after classification, it was only a matter of time before you would have to face the "Welcome Wagon" and be challenged to pay or to fight.

The Welcome Wagon visited me shortly after I arrived at Graterford. I was sitting in the movie theater. In those days, prison recreational staff didn't have videotapes, so they showed films in large auditoriums. It gets pretty dark there. I was watching the movie when suddenly I felt this sharp knife on my throat. The guy wasn't asking me for a match! Four or five inmates behind me started talking about how they wanted money and they wanted it quickly. I felt completely helpless, surrounded and isolated as I sat frozen in my seat. Somehow, I had the presence of mind to ask them how much they wanted and when, so I could have it dressed up and ready to go. That strategy bought me some time. About two days later, I met the Welcome Wagon again in the auditorium, but this time I was prepared to fight.

Once the movie had ended and most of the movie-going inmates had left the auditorium, the lights were turned on and I could see four of the extortionists cautiously inching toward me from different directions. I stood tense for battle in plain view in the center of the room with my back against a wall, daring them to come closer. I had a big deadly looking shank in each of my outstretched hands and my pockets were full of ground black pepper I could use as mace to temporarily blind anyone who tried to rush me. As I hoped, this bluff worked and the Welcome Wagon carefully retreated out of the auditorium, more than a little worried I might decide to go after them. After this, they left me alone, preferring easier game.

These were violent and deadly times at Graterford, times of random murders, cell fires, paranoia, and knife carrying. According to the Department of Corrections' Monthly Morbidity Report in 1986–1987, Graterford accounted for the highest rate of assaults of Pennsylvania's twelve state prisons: 392 assaults by inmates against inmates and 47 by inmates against staff, a total of 439.

While it seemed like total anarchy, it really wasn't. This was mob rule with a purpose, a throwback to a time long before civilized man developed modern social institutions. By now I began to realize how fragile civilization was and how easily modern man could be reduced to the savagery of his prehistoric ancestors. Although we had TVs, radios, clothes, and a wealth of commissary goods, behaviorally we had regressed thousands of years backward on the social evolutionary scale. The man (or men) with the biggest club ruled. The new order was now the law of the jungle.

Violence in Graterford had also become a form of escape for many inmates. In creating and maintaining a predatory environment, these men were able to avoid the reality of imprisonment by focusing all their attention on fighting one another. The more hostile the environment, the more they saw themselves as victims and the less responsible they felt for their own actions. This obsession with violence became as destructive as any narcotic addiction.

People caught up in this violent escapism never perceived it as their reaction to incarceration, any more than I could see the danger of oversleeping before it was pointed out to me. Sadly, the ones who ended up suffering the most were those who came to prison just to pay their debt to society—those who hoped one day to return to their lives in the mainstream. They suffered twice: once at the hands of the predatory inmates and then again through the prison's system of punishment.

Another contributing factor to this upsurge of violence was the creation of new subcultures within the prison. These arose from the new types of inmates who had now extended the roster of victims and predators in the general population. People who in the past would never have been committed to an adult correction facility were now queuing up for their "three hots and a cot" in ever-increasing numbers.

Many of these were the mentally ill who had spilled out of state mental hospitals, which had been closed down in the seventies. These "nuts," as inmates simply called them, were pathetic and destructive. Their illnesses made punishment in the normal sense virtually impossible. Their helplessness often made them the favorite victims of predatory inmates. Worst of all, their special needs and peculiar behavior destroyed the stability of the prison system.

There were also growing numbers of the homeless as well as juvenile offenders committed as adults. But the largest group of new arrivals were young, minority drug dealers and users, most of them from inner-city ghettos.

When the homeless came to Graterford, they were just looking for a secure haven from the streets. They weren't interested in counselors, treatment, or discipline. They had no sense of their own criminality. Juveniles suffered the most. They viewed prison as a surrogate parent and so expected to be protected and sheltered. What they got instead was victimization by adult inmates and indifferent bureaucrats. Finally, the drug addicts and dealers saw Graterford as one more rehab center to dry them up and help them overcome their habit. Few thought of themselves as criminals because they perceived themselves as the victims of their own addictions.

Like me, all these newcomers sought to have their needs met. But Graterford, a maximum-security prison, could not identify these needs, let alone meet them. A prison confines, punishes, and sometimes deters. It is neither designed nor inclined to foster, cure, or rehabilitate. In meeting only the basic needs of the new arrivals (food, shelter, clothing, and medical care), Graterford's resources were stretched beyond its limits. Additionally, many of the guards and treatment staff, who were accustomed to supplying inmates with only a minimum amount of services and a maximum amount of discipline, were embittered by the fact that these new arrivals were coming into the prison with expectations of treatment and care.

Soon, the mentally ill were commanding too much of the staff's attention. Drug addicts, many of them going through withdrawal, were doing anything they could to get high. Juveniles were being raped and causing havoc trying to attract some "parental" attention. Because of all this, instead of changing people, Graterford itself was changing. Because most of the new commitments came from blighted urban areas, the changes often reflected that environment.

This fear and violence had changed Graterford as profoundly as it had changed me. The new prison subcultures with their disrespect for authority, drug addiction, illiteracy, and welfare mentality had altered the institution's very character. All the evils of the decaying American inner city were being compressed into one overcrowded prison.

Ironically, the violence that had long been a tool of control by the administration was now being used against it to send its prison system hurtling out of control. Much of the violence that invaded Graterford in the 1980s was actually imported from the streets by the social misfits who were now being called convicts. They were criminals before—the only change in their identity is that now they're incarcerated, lost their names, and were assigned numbers. For many of these newcomers, prison violence was simply life as usual.

Reacting to this new environment, the Old Heads would tell anyone who would listen about the "good old days." The typical Old Head had come to Graterford a decade or more earlier after spending most of his life behind bars. What puzzled me and others my age was how these seasoned prison elders would pine over the rigidly structured routine, solitude, mistreatment, and hard labor of those good old days. When asked about it, they would talk about times when the outside world was kept outside, when an inmate's natural enemies were the guards, and when men did extraordinary things to go home.

Now those good old days had become a bygone era. To the Old Heads, prison life today lacked the honor, quiet solitude, and routine that had once made incarceration more noble. Now the greatest threat to an inmate had become other inmates, particularly the "Young Bucks" who had infested the general population. With their ruthless and reckless selfishness, Young Bucks relentlessly challenged the established routine and order of both convicts and staff, so that the stability and relative peace Old Heads had established and now enjoyed were being replaced by chaos and mayhem.

An example of this new threat was the way debts were collected. Old Heads were always careful to whom they gave credit. If a debtor fell behind in payments, the debt was usually doubled and any of his belongings would be taken as collateral. Physical violence was employed only as a last resort. In contrast, the Young Bucks would lend anything to anybody. Should a debtor be late in paying, even if it was a single pack of cigarettes, he would immediately be beaten and robbed.

It seemed almost as if these compulsive youths were more interested in committing violence than in making money. This all too common practice of swift punishment for indebtedness disturbed the Old Heads' sense of fair play. "Working from the muscle" was to them unsound business, but the Young Bucks would have it no other way. To the Old Heads nothing in business was personal, but to the young newcomers *everything* was personal.

What disturbed the Old Heads most was how these newcomers had so readily and completely accepted prison as their life. Everything they did, including using and dealing drugs, smuggling contraband, forming violent gangs, and embracing homosexuality, was undertaken to make themselves more comfortable *in* prison—not to get *out* of prison. Few of them challenged their convictions in court and still fewer contemplated escape. They were too busy enjoying themselves.

This confounded the Old Heads, who could not conceive of a life beyond the walls so oppressive that it would cause all these strong and able-bodied young men to forfeit their freedom so willingly. Nor could the Old Heads win in their losing battle against the new prison subculture of Young Bucks who fought for prison turf as if it were their birthright.

To illustrate this conflict between generations, one of my closest Old Head friends was released from prison the day after he had slapped a Young Buck in the prison yard because "he didn't know how to talk to a man." Some time after his release, my friend was shot to death in a bar by that same young man, who had recklessly sought revenge beyond the prison walls with no regard for the consequences. The assassin has since been caught and now sits on death row.

By 1984, years after I had lost my clerical job, I was working as an infirmary janitor. Stabbings, murders, and serious injuries had become so frequent that the medical staff created a special unit, to which I was assigned. Our job was to respond to the medical emergencies on the general population blocks.

They called us the "Meat Wagon Crew." When summoned, we would rush to the scene of a medical emergency, a staff nurse in the lead, one inmate pushing a gurney, another carrying an emergency medical kit, and a third bearing oxygen or medical equipment. Although our crew was originally intended to serve as an ambulance service, it in fact more closely resembled a coroner's wagon. Two or three times a week, we could be seen rushing through the many long concrete corridors in response to an emergency call. Often we arrived only in time to remove a dead body or the unconscious victim of an assault.

In one case, an inmate had died of a drug overdose. He sat frozen on his bed, his lifeless eyes staring out a window. Inattentive (or poorly trained) guards simply added him to their usual count, while passing inmates wondered what could be so interesting outside. Finally, someone asked the stiff body that question, only to discover that dead men don't talk. When the Meat Wagon arrived, we had to struggle to get the rigid corpse out of the cell's narrow opening to the waiting gurney.

In most cases, if the medical emergency didn't involve a drug overdose, it was usually some aftermath of violence. One inmate, who had been attacked over nonpayment of a two-cigarette-pack debt, was found with his intestines spilling out from a razor slash across his stomach. We had to keep pushing his entrails back into place as we raced the gurney down the corridor. Another man's face had been so badly beaten that I didn't recognize him as one of my friends until a guard identified him from his ID card.

By 1985, the body count was so high that we stopped running to answer our calls. The helpless victimization of our fellow inmates and our own frustration eventually rendered us indifferent to violence. Violence or degradation, self-defense or lost self-esteem, kill or be killed—these are not real choices. In the same way, Graterford offered no real choices to the multitude of men overcrowded within its walls. The violence of inmates was no worse than the brutality and insensitivity of an indifferent, omnipotent bureaucracy. In the long run, Graterford's great walls would never be high enough to contain the hatred, violence, and rage swelling out of proportion inside.

9

Friends in Low Places

It is hard to find friends in prison because most inmates are anti-social by disposition or through prison conditioning. One of the cruelest aspects of a penitentiary is the way it leaves one isolated and lonely despite the overcrowded and violent surroundings. Yet, because of all the fear and hardship we experienced together, the friends I made at Graterford turned out to be my closest. The harsher the conditions, the closer the bonds between us.

TONY: IT HAPPENS ALL THE TIME

Tony was my neighbor at Graterford. I met him the first day I entered general population. He was a tall, rectangular man who cast an imposing shadow. His thick, black, well-trimmed beard with neatly groomed hair gave his block of a body a crown of sophistication.

"If you need to know anything about this joint, just ask me," he told me as I sorted through my belongings. "My name's Tony. I live a few cells down."

There was much that I needed to know about my new home, and Tony was more than willing to instruct me. He had read about my case in the newspaper and knew I had a background in law, which motivated him to be as helpful as possible. Nothing is free in prison, and the price for Tony's friendship was my assistance with some criminal cases he was appealing.

Tony was a jailhouse lawyer. Every morning, he hung a paper sign in front of his cell that announced *LEGAL AID.* His cell was arranged like a small office. The steel desk mounted on one side had all the necessary office supplies and adornments, including a manual typewriter. Alongside his desk was a makeshift chair assembled out of stacked boxes and old newspapers. The chair stood by the entrance to his cell, so a "client" did not have to enter too far to conduct business. On a shelf above his desk and peppered throughout his cell were thick law books to punctuate his "profession."

Tony was admittedly no legal wizard. When asked what he did for a living, he would proudly and without hesitation reply, "I rob banks." Helping people out with their legal work kept him busy and his cell filled with commissary items. He was doing fifteen to thirty years so he had plenty of time to occupy.

Tony was a well-disciplined man with streetwise intelligence, so he had managed to teach himself enough about the law to handle legal issues and fill out appeal forms. However, he lacked the ability to properly litigate an appeal to its end. With most cases, he would read an inmate's transcripts, fill out an appropriated appeal form, and then have the court appoint a real attorney for his client. The charge for these services would amount to what he felt the client could afford, from a pack of commissary cigarettes to a couple of hundred dollars.

Tony functioned as effectively as any legal secretary I had ever known and provided a needed service. Many of the men at Graterford were illiterate, and the only way for them to begin the process of appealing their convictions was with the services of a jailhouse lawyer. In reality, most collateral appeals filed on behalf of inmates are the product of jailhouse lawyers—a poor man's last-ditch effort for justice. As one can imagine, some jailhouse lawyers are honest and qualified, while others are con men hoping to hustle inmates out of money, often ruining their chances for a successful appeal. The caveat *Buyer Beware* holds true in prison as well.

To his credit, Tony was reliable and made up in enthusiasm what he lacked in legal expertise. As my own jailhouse legal practice began to thrive, I often referred minor cases like parole violations and guilty pleas to his able office. This spared me most of the nuisance cases and made Tony very happy. Once I became his neighbor, his clientele doubled and he gained a few pounds from all the commissary cakes and candies he was earning.

Every morning before I went about my business, I stopped at Tony's cell, sat on his client's chair, and enjoyed his offer of hot instant coffee and commissary pastry. Tony and I chatted for a half hour or more about legal issues, the prison, or anything else on our minds. It was always a good way to start off a morning.

In the afternoons, I performed my assigned prison job as a janitor in the infirmary. At times, I was asked by one of the nurses to escort her to the Special Needs Unit. This unit was a small caged-in section of the infirmary where the seriously mentally ill were housed. It was a dark, bleak place where men resembling zombies spent their days sitting or pacing, waiting for meals or medications. These inmates were not allowed outdoors for exercise, and some had spent years inside this forgotten purgatory.

Female nurses often preferred to be accompanied by an inmate janitor during their rounds in this ward for their own safety. In turn, janitors enjoyed the chance to serve as escorts, as it gave them an opportunity to flirt with a female. Men will be men, after all, and I was no exception.

As requested, I carried a tray of medication and walked behind the nurse toward the Special Needs Unit, referred to as "D-Rear." The guard assigned to D-Rear unlocked a wire-mesh gate and allowed us into the dark, dirty, foul-smelling cage.

Ghoulishly assembled around a large table were about twenty inmates eagerly awaiting their meds. Men of all colors, sizes, and shapes stared with wide-eyed expectation for the nurse to call out their name. Each inmate slowly shuffled over to the nurse, who handed him his medication. I gave him a paper cup of water with which to down his meds, and then he moved away into the darkness to wait for the drug to spirit him away into his own netherworld.

It was such a sad sight. I could never wait to get out of there, nor did I wish to be reminded that places like this existed. When the nurse finished, she asked me to follow her to a new patient who was unable to walk. Reluctantly, I trailed deeper into the bowels of D-Rear.

Somewhere in a far corner sat a lone man obscured by shadows. Everyone else was walking a slow, tedious circle around the ward for daily recreation. It was too dark for me to be able to identify the man. I looked away as the nurse gave him his medication. She asked me for water. I approached and extended a water cup—only to be shocked by the sight of Tony, sitting motionless, drool oozing from his mouth.

"Tony, that can't be you!" I called out in astonishment. I had done my usual morning coffee and chat with this man less than eight hours ago. "This must be some kind of mistake," I told myself.

The nurse saw my alarm as I tried to arouse Tony. "He can't hear you, Victor. He's on too much medication. Is he a friend of yours?"

I wanted to tell her about Tony, what a smart guy he was, the efficient, little office he had in the cell, and the way he never took advantage of people. But I couldn't. All I could do was stare at this shell of a man who slumped silently before me. "Yes, he is," was all I could say.

The nurse ushered me out of the unit. My body followed, but my eyes remained fixed on Tony.

"Look, there's nothing you can do for him," the nurse advised. "He's really out there right now."

"What happened?"

"No one really knows. I got a call to report to the block to pick up an inmate and take him to the infirmary. When I got to his cell, your friend was lying on his bed, mumbling gibberish and repeating that he couldn't do the time. He wasn't violent or anything. He was pretty much like you saw him. Do you know if he got some bad news about anything?"

"No," I answered, although I had no way of knowing. "What's going to happen to him?" I asked in a delayed panic. "What can I do?"

"Calm down, Victor. There's nothing you can do. The doctors will treat him. And soon he'll be back out in population. He'll probably have to stay on some kind of medication. There's lots of guys who go through this and they come around eventually. It happens all the time."

Years later, I filed a class action lawsuit against Graterford and the Department of Corrections, challenging among other things the conditions in D-Rear. A federal judge, after inspecting D-Rear, declared it an unfit place for human beings. Shortly thereafter, D-Rear was discontinued and a licensed mental health group arrived to operate an independent Special Needs Unit inside Graterford. When the new mental health unit finally opened, I said a little prayer for my friend Tony and all the others who "couldn't do the time."

DAVID: A SEXUAL VICTIM

When I first met David he was starting a two- to five-year sentence, and I was two years into my life sentence. David was nineteen then and "cute as a button"—a curse for any young man in prison. At the time, I was working as a clerk in the Chapel, which was how I met him. It was there that he was assaulted and raped repeatedly by at least three prisoners. I was present to see the aftermath of young David's introduction into Graterford's criminal justice system, one of many lessons on the facts of life in prison.

David was gang-raped not once, but twice. Now in his late twenties, he has served close to half his life in institutions and has made most of the important decisions of his life based on the experience interacting with inmates. David's story, a grim portrait of today's incarcerated youth, presents a too-common slice of prison life that is sadder than that of many of the broken men who are my neighbors, and sadder still than the prison pallor that greets me in the mirror every morning. The following is excerpted from a conversation I had with David.

"When I got to Graterford, I took protective custody lockup twenty-four hours a day. A guard came down one day who had a pass for me to go get legal mail. He unlocked my door and left. I got up out of bed in my underwear and was rushed by approximately six or more inmates. I was raped numerous times. They rushed me, then threw me to the floor and hit me a few times. Before I had a chance to react, a knife was placed at my neck. I was already on my side or stomach. I don't remember what was said. I somewhat knew what they wanted and it wasn't my commissary.

"All they did was fuck me with no emotion. I was hoping while this was happening that they would ask me to have oral sex and I would then bite them. Had it been under other circumstances, I would have fought back. At that time I was in good shape. I would guess logically that it was a 'set up.' They left as soon as it was over. I was angry, bleeding, and in quite a bit of pain. Because I was in protective custody and it happened there, telling or reporting it was pointless and also very dangerous....

"I lost all hope for about six months. I was totally stripped of emotion. I just didn't give a fuck anymore. When I was much younger, I was a vengeful person. But I didn't want to get even because where there is an action, there is always a reaction....

"After the first time I was raped while in protective custody, I convinced the officials to let me out in population without telling them that I was assaulted. They let me out into population and I ran into a friend who I met on the street. I hung around with him for a while, figuring he could teach me the ropes of survival in the 'Big House.' He introduced me to a fellow who was too nice, who one day invited me to the Chapel to get high. I met him, and he had a few friends with him. We smoked a couple of joints, and the next thing I knew I was getting physically beaten and again was viciously raped by at least three guys. . . .

"After I was raped, the only medical attention that I received was a physical examination of my rectum to confirm that I had been assaulted. I was placed back in protective custody by myself without anyone to talk to, alone and deserted like a dirty rag. I received no therapy from either a psychologist or a psychiatrist. I was left to deal with it on my own.

"I didn't cry out then because no one seemed to care, and so I stripped myself of all and any emotions. If there were people who cared, they really didn't come forward, which is natural, because it is a very difficult thing to respond to. I can sympathize with women victims. It is a devastating experience to not only cope with, but even more to live with. . . .

"Once I was released from prison, I was very demanding of people because I felt they owed me something. And more than often, if my wishes were not complied with, I took what I desired from them. Don't get me wrong, I never raped anyone, but I did lash out on all the supposed predators and even those, both family and friends, who I felt deserved to be tormented. I didn't discriminate. I did it to anyone I felt had it coming to them. Anyway, that was how sick I was then, or rather that was how obsessed I was, until recently. Now, mostly I feel guilty about what I've done in an act of retaliation. But I also realize I was really crying for help in the only way I could, by acting out.

"I am a very confused person now, sexually that is, because I am insecure about what is natural combined with what I've been through and seen with my own eyes through the many years that I've been in institutions, thirteen years altogether. I am attracted to younger guys because of their innocent look and naive personalities, more so because it's that very innocence that I was robbed of.

"Sometimes I feel really guilty after I have sex with a guy, because I know or feel that I have violated their minds subconsciously, and eventually they'll have to face the music about who they are or cop out and remain a victim. But I am realizing that all that is happening is that I am doing it because that's the only way I can get any kind of love, affection, and attention that I so desperately need. [As for the system], I still don't trust them because they are the true predators and rapers of the people."

Rape is no longer a random act of violence that occurs occasionally in prison: it is now a common event behind bars, across all facilities. Few inmates today are free from the fear of rape. The strong and the weak, gang members and loners, cautious inmates and reckless ones all are potential victims of violent, uninhibited inmates in violent, overcrowded prisons. Sexual assaults are so pervasive in correctional facilities today that they have become unspoken, de facto parts of court-imposed punishments.

The culprit behind the explosion of prison rape is prison overcrowding. Since the late 1970s, the nationwide prison population has more than tripled. (In Pennsylvania the population has more than quadrupled.) Prison managers have faced the immediate concerns of housing, clothing, and feeding the flood of men, women, and even children who were suddenly being sent to prison. Meeting these basic human needs continues to be a daily challenge for prison administrators, who find themselves without the necessary resources to maintain adequate living conditions, let alone to protect inmates from each other. With overcrowding, prison rape has evolved from an unspeakable act of depraved violence into a key strategy in the fight for dominance, complete with its own sophisticated techniques. In the process, prison rapists have been elevated from the status of degenerates into shrewd predators admired for their tactics.

In an effort to reduce the skyrocketing costs of operating overcrowded prisons, state legislatures have imposed fiscal restraints on prison spending, often including hiring freezes. As a result, the inmate-to-staff ratio in most prisons has increased. This reduction in prison employee hiring has significantly contributed to the increase in violence that now plagues many prisons. Administrators found themselves forced to implement untested inmate management practices and procedures to deal with overcrowding. One of the most significant and disastrous of the new policies was the practice of putting two or more inmates in a prison cell specifically designed for single occupancy.

Recent inmate employment policies have also contributed. Before overcrowding, every able-bodied inmate was required to work. But when prison administrators found themselves with more inmates than available jobs, the policy of total inmate employment was modified. Current prison policy defines inmate work as a privilege that only the deserving are entitled to receive. A large percentage of inmates have been left idle and impoverished as a result of this new employment policy. The practical consequence is the creation of a large underclass of unemployed and desperate inmates, who engage in endless mischief to generate income and keep busy.

The problem with stopping prison rapists is only compounded because victims of rape are reluctant to report the crime to authorities. This silence spares cost-conscious prison officials the expense and the burden of investigating and prosecuting incidents of prison rape. Prisons are not designed to administer justice; the primary job of prison administrators is to maintain order and discipline while preventing escapes. Therefore, when a victim reports a rape to prison authorities, both the victim and the rapist will immediately be locked in isolation under different statuses (protective custody for the victim; disciplinary custody for the offender). Despite these different statuses, the victim and the offender get the same basic treatment. Rapists are thus virtually handed licenses for their attacks.

Also, it appears that prison staff members have recently relaxed their attitudes about the rape of inmates. Some staff members now seem to view prison rape as a part of the punishment risk that lawbreakers take when they commit their crimes. Others see it simply as retribution carried out on an interpersonal level: if a homosexual gets raped, staff may believe that she or he deserved it.

Prison violence, and especially rape, thrive in this climate of chronic double celling, dormitory housing, unemployment, lax security, poor facility design (blind spots), and poor management. In prisons today, rapists have their free pick of victims like David. He is getting out of prison again soon. I wonder whether he will find that desperately needed love, affection, and attention in the outside world. And if he doesn't, I wonder what he will do.

CHASER: A MEDICATION ADDICT

I met Chaser in 1984, my fourth year at Graterford, when he first arrived to serve time on a robbery conviction. I can still remember the frightened look on his face that first day. As I was adapting to the rapidly changing rules and conditions of a prison in total meltdown, Chaser became the beneficiary of my hard-learned lessons on inmate survival. We managed to forge a mutual friendship.

Many outsiders who have met Chaser would comment, "He doesn't look like he belongs in here." I've heard this often when people encounter an inmate who doesn't have some grotesque feature that neatly fits their preconceived notion of the "criminal look." Experience has taught me that the less an inmate appears like a criminal, the more likely he is to be particularly vicious and unrepentant. Criminals who look like criminals keep people on guard; the honest-looking ones put them at ease, which allows them the greater advantage of misjudgment. But in Chaser's case they were right. He didn't belong in prison, let alone deserve to become a victim of the system.

I did my best to look after my friend until, about nine months later, he was transferred to the Rockview facility. This was a relief for me, because protecting a naive and scared young man from the predators at Graterford was no easy task. What Chaser and I didn't know at the time was that prison administrators were feverishly trying to figure out how to stop the imminent collapse of Graterford and other overcrowded prisons. With thousands of new, young Chasers coming in, it was becoming impossible to feed, house, and clothe them all, let alone rehabilitate them.

More important to officials, an increasing number of guards and staff were becoming victims of inmate attacks. As employee safety was their first priority, the administrators realized that something had to be done to shore up the cracks in Graterford's foundation—and it had to be quick, cheap, and effective. But Chaser and I never concerned ourselves with the administration's problems. After all, we had swag men to deal with and predators to avoid.

In 1990, after I too had been transferred to Rockview, I ran into Chaser again and talked about life in Graterford. He was walking out of the dining hall's special section reserved for the nuts, whom the administration refer to euphemistically as "special-needs inmates." Chaser walked sluggishly with a disheveled, glassy-eyed appearance. In short, he *looked* like one of the nuts.

"Chaser, is that you?" I asked.

"Hey, Vic," he replied, "I've got to talk to you. It's real important. Meet me in the yard."

That evening in the yard, my old friend explained to me how he had returned to the streets two years earlier, only to lose his wife and son, develop a voracious drug habit, and end up committing burglaries to support his habit. I was unmoved by Chaser's story, because almost every returning con I've ever met recounts a similar tale of woe. All I wanted to know was why he was on the nut block and why he was taking "brake fluid" (prescribed psychotropic medication). It was obvious because of his very slow, disjointed movement and his shakes. Another alarming clue was the noticeable scars on his wrists from razor cuts.

Chaser described how his return to prison had exposed him to the "medicate-and-forget-them" system of modern prison management. This new system of mind-altering and mood-altering psychotropic drugs was rapidly becoming the prison administration's "quick, cheap (psychotropic drugs are expensive, so instead of cheap, I would say effortless), and effective" solution to warehousing masses of inmates into smaller spaces, while using fewer and fewer support services.

The reasoning seemed to be that every dose of medication taken by an inmate equaled one less fraction of a guard needed to watch that inmate and one less inmate who may pose a threat to anyone other than himself. Hence, overcrowding had brought about a merging of the psychiatric and corrections communities. The resulting effect on inmates can be best described by Chaser during our following conversation.

"The first time [I came to prison] I was terrified because I didn't know what to expect and I knew no one. I was awkward and didn't know my way around. I had not acquired a prison or inmate mentality. The second time I was much more at ease because I knew a lot of people still in prison and I knew what to expect. I had also learned quite fast how to become as comfortable as possible. I had to take a lot of psychotropic drugs to achieve this comfortable state of mind. . . .

"In November of 1989, after telling the shrink in the county prison that I wished I was dead, I was unknowingly given Sinequan, which knocked me out for three days. But since I was in a special quiet section of the jail, I continued the medication, because to me it was better than being in population. . . .

"I think the biggest difference between street drugs and psychotropic drugs is that street drugs give me some kind of feeling of well-being, high, confidence, euphoria, and contentment. But psychotropic drugs cause all feeling to cease. It stops self-awareness and sucks the soul out of a man. It slows or stops a man from striving to better himself and he stops caring about everything. It also creates total laziness. That laziness becomes his entire attitude and also is 100 percent habit-forming....

"After almost three months at the county prison in Philly, I was sent to Graterford to start my four- to ten-year sentence. I had abruptly stopped taking the Sinequan and felt totally disoriented. I lasted three weeks in population. Looking for drugs, I ended up taking another inmate's Thorazine at times. I was out of control and all I could think of or look forward to was getting stoned.

"One day I got very drunk and went into a blackout and refused to lock up. Four guards carried me to a room and I was put into restraints. I was given nine months in the Hole. I did five at Graterford and was sent to Rockview to complete it....

"[Getting medication in Rockview] was quite easy. I said I wished I was dead, which was the same thing I said in the county. Every week the shrink would ask, 'How do you feel now?' All I had to do was say, 'Bad,' and ask for more or different meds. I always got what I asked for, as long as I told them I thought of killing myself....

"I took Sinequan, Mellaril, Elavil, Klonopin, first separately, while always asking for Valium. Then in desperation, I mixed the medications and the dosages. The ultimate effect was total numbness. My body was numb. My feelings were numb, and then my mind was numb. I did not care what happened to me and just stopped thinking about anything....

"While taking the meds, I was put on a special block and given a single cell. I got only a reprimand at misconduct hearings and did not have to go to work. I felt I was being placated and given special attention and I liked that. But when I stopped taking the meds, I was shook down [cell-searched] a lot and went to the Hole if I was ever given a misconduct. Once in the Hole, I would say I wish I was dead, and again they'd give me medication....

"I admitted to staff many times that I had a severe drug addiction and that I had an abusive personality. I tried numerous times to get in the drug-therapy groups and on the D- and A- [Drug and Alcohol] Blocks. I was refused and ignored every time. . . .

"I lost all sense of dignity and self-worth. I had no pride. I lost all interest in the outside world and eventually did not care if I ever returned to it. All I knew or cared about was what times I went to get my fix. . . . [I] hurried to be first in line. I constantly had the shakes and inner tremors. My speech was slurred and slowed, and so was my thinking. I could not think ahead. I was like a small child only looking for instant gratification. My entire metabolism changed, and I gained a lot of weight fast. It damaged my memory, even to this day. . . .

"Since I was under constant supervision and being evaluated once or twice a month, pre-release and parole became much harder to obtain. So for the luxury of being comfortable and in a fantasy world, I had to abandon the idea of early release or furloughs. Since my number-one priority was no longer a goal, it became easy for me to forget or stop striving for what was once important to me.

"The side effects of the medication, such as tremors and shakes, made it impossible for me to get and keep a job. Education, reading, learning, and working to strengthen my mind became things of the past. Giving up became repetitious and habit-forming (not unlike street drugs) and eventually I lost and gave up my self-respect, dignity, and morals until my only interest in life was getting in line three times a day to receive my medication.

"I had given up on all these things, and I woke up one day and realized I was a very sad man. But I was willing to give up on life, because the medications I was taking made me think I was comfortable. . . . I had given up on Chaser. . . .

"I was seeing a shrink two times a week because I was depressed. I was not diagnosed as having any kind of mental illness or chemical imbalance, but despite that I was taking large dosages of Thorazine, Sinequan, lithium, Elavil, and Melloril. I took them at 7 am, 11 am, 4 pm, 8 pm. . . .

"One night just before lockup, I got another misconduct. I didn't care if I went to the Hole or got cell restriction. What concerned me was that the administration might possibly take away my medication. So after weighing my options, it seemed only logical to kill myself, or at the least, give that appearance. I opened my window, pressed my wrists against the frozen bars, then took an old razor and opened my wrists.

I figured that, if I died, that would be fine. But, if I lived, I would definitely get more medication, and that thought satisfied me.

"I lived this madness and insanity for well over a year, until I ran into you. You offered me your time and energy to explain to me what I was doing to myself and what I was becoming. Within six months, I was totally off the special-needs block and off 99 percent of the medication and my will to live and succeed returned with a vengeance. I never needed the medications for my depressed condition. I just needed someone to say they cared. I needed a friend. I got both from you. I owe you my life, not the prison, and not the medication....

"I have been medication-free for two years now and, although I'm usually uncomfortable with prison conditions, I can look in the mirror and see Chaser looking back with a smile. So to me, giving up the medication was a small price to pay to be myself again.

"[Psychotropic medication] is one of the easiest things to get in prison. It is easier to go to the shrink and ask for 500 mg of Thorazine than it is to get on the phone or get a pass to the Chapel. If a guy goes to the doc saying he feels depressed, violent, or suicidal, the doc will give him one of numerous medications. He is usually given a choice. All the medications are geared to slow a man down or fog his thinking so bad he can't think of why he's depressed, violent, or suicidal. This will continue for years, as long as he says he needs the medications to a staff person once a month....

"I'd say 40 percent of the population here is taking some form of psychotropic medication. They are treated less harshly than those unmedicated. They are seen and talked to by staff much more often than those not on medications. They are given special consideration at misconduct hearings. They are permitted to come in from night yard earlier than the other inmates and, in a lot of cases, are given a single cell. When it comes to working, someone on psychotropic medication can usually pick whatever job he says he can handle. On the other hand, most of us were not required to work at all....

"I believe that, when a guard or any staff member puts on a uniform, they know it stands for authority. So they demand respect and control. When someone rebels or stands up to them, they feel their authority and control is threatened and they take steps to eliminate the rebellion. They put on the appearance of power, so they act cold, mean, negative, and harsh to display this power.

"Now when a guy is on medication, the threat is almost nonexistent. They [the staff] feel safe and secure with the men that are medicated. So the use of force and display of power is not necessary, and they act more leniently to the medicated inmate. They treat these men like children. To staff, a medicated inmate is a controlled inmate....

"[If all inmates were required to take psychotropic drugs], I would be shocked and scared. It would be like they were turning the prison into a brainwashing institution. I would think they had lost all control and were attempting to gain it back by stopping our wills and brains from functioning properly. I believe they are headed in that direction because of how easy the medications are to get and how many people are taking them....

"I think that, as the prison populations continue to grow and grow, and a younger and more violent crowd comes in, it will become harder and harder for the administration to control all the blocks. I think they are now learning that the best way to control inmates or pacify them is to totally medicate them. It may even become a reward system."

Psychotropic drugs are nothing new to the psychiatric community, which has been using them on the mentally ill for years. However, its use in corrections as a population-management tool and behavior modifier is relatively new. The effects of prolonged use of such medication on an ever-growing number of inmates are unknown. Just from the increasing size of medication lines and the growing number of inmates doing the brake-fluid shuffle, I have observed that psychotropic medications (also known as "chemical shackles") are defining the behavior of an increasing percentage of inmates in the general population.

As politicians and bureaucrats continue to debate the loftier issues facing the criminal justice system, the mother of invention has required front-line prison administrators to quickly implement any practice that might help them to keep their prisons intact and functioning. The practice of medicating inmates is becoming popular because it has proven to be a relatively inexpensive and efficient prison-control tool. The two governing estates of custody and treatment are being pushed aside by the rising third estate of psychiatric medication.

A bureaucratic system that subdues whole populations with drugs must certainly give us pause. The wisdom of turning means into ultimate ends in this way needs to be questioned. Today in prison, I find myself longing for any glimpse of an attempt to rehabilitate, not because I believe that treatment works, but because I worry about a society that no longer cares enough to try to help.

In my opinion, today's prison managers are only interested in their ability to confine an ever-increasing number of people for an ever-longer period of time. Because there is only so much that can be done in terms of cell and prison design, the search for solutions has focused not on changing the nature of prisons but on changing the nature of prisoners.

As of this interview, Chaser has been off medication for about two years. He has successfully gone through drug-rehabilitation therapy and is soon due for release. Once released, he will join a growing number of mind-altered men who are leaving prison and entering the mainstream of society. Only time will tell whether chemically treated inmates do in fact make law-abiding citizens. But, if you ask me, we should go back to trying to build a better mousetrap and, for God's sake, leave the mice alone.

DOUBLE D AND ROCKY

Dan, my chess companion and one of my earliest friends at Graterford, was a quiet, soft-spoken man who stood a tall six feet and weighed about 180 pounds. His prison handle was Double D, an abbreviation for Dangerous Dan. I had met Double D when I was in the county jail awaiting trial. For some reason he took a liking to me. I would prefer to think it was because of my dynamic personality, charm, and wit, but in prison such qualities don't count for much. Chances are, he liked me because he felt I was of some use to him. I've never really been certain why, but whatever the reason, I valued his friendship highly in those early years.

Dan never talked much, didn't lie, didn't steal, and didn't mince words. Although he belonged to no prison gang, he was respected by everyone. Those who didn't respect him feared him to the very marrow of their bones. We both loved chess and, while he was a much better opponent, I played well enough for him to enjoy beating me. We played a lot on the block, because I didn't like being too far away from my cell. The good thing about chess is that it's not a spectator sport and is so boring to watch that it kept people away. Dan and

I were able to have long, leisurely games and conversations without distraction.

"Why do they call you 'Dangerous'?" I once asked.

"Because they know I won't take any shit from any of these fleas."

"A lot of guys are afraid of you."

Dan rubbed his forehead and pushed up the brim of his ever-present prison work cap. Its tightly creased brim stood at a crisp forty-five degrees to the ceiling, moving around like the dorsal fin of a shark. After a long silence, he replied, "I like it like that."

I must confess that being a friend of Double D's had certain advantages. One was the freedom to play chess without ever having to worry about an ambush or an attack, fairly common events in those days. Once while we were playing, a mountain of a brute walked by. Dan never looked up, but I could sense he was watching the man's every move. I could also sense there was no love lost between them.

Rocky was the biggest and toughest convict in Graterford, and inmates and staff alike paid deference to him. He led a gang of black and white thugs called the "Terminators," which he liked to refer to as a paramilitary organization of anti-government terrorists. I had been told that Rocky's Terminators were the largest gang of extortionists, drug dealers, and smugglers in the prison. But to Double D, "Rocky's just another flea."

"You don't like him?" I asked one day after I made a rather stupid chess move.

"No. Pay attention to the board," Dan said in that soft voice.

"Why do you think they let him do the shit he does?"

Dan gritted his teeth with annoyance and rubbed his forehead, the shark fin of his cap circling the air. "Because he works for the prison. He's doing exactly what they want him to."

I had played enough chess with Double D to know his words were as complicated as his chess strategy. "What do you mean?"

The fin came toward me. "This place only lets happen what it wants to happen. Rocky's no bigger than the three hundred guards they got working here. That silly Terminator stuff is just bullshit. They use Rocky to keep everybody in line. He does their dirty work." Then he proceeded to beat me mercilessly on the chessboard, as if to emphasize his point.

According to Double D, Graterford had gone through some violent changes in the 1970s. Despite its rigidity and strict military discipline, three staff members had been murdered. One was a captain of the guard who in 1979 had had his head split open by a baseball bat in the main corridor. By the early 1980s, prison gangs had become firmly entrenched and the administration did not have the manpower or the know-how to deal with them. Furthermore, the rigidity and discipline did nothing to make their jobs any easier.

So, as Dan saw it, the administration decided to play a gambit: They relaxed the rules and, instead of trying to end the gangs, they manipulated them by playing one against the other. In this way gangs would be too busy fighting each other to work together against the system. To destabilize these gangs, the administration threw its support behind one gang to maintain a balance of power. So Rocky's Terminators became the administration's flavor of the month.

To me, this seemed too far-fetched to be the product of any rational administrative policy. Besides, it sounded illegal; you can't support corruption if you're paid to combat it. But in those days I knew very little about the prison system. So I discounted Double D's story, reasoning that the Terminators' success was more likely due to the result of administrative ineptitude. The staff was simply as frightened of Rocky as were most of the inmates.

"Rocky's going to get himself killed," volunteered Double D one day, as he murdered me on the chess board.

"Why do you say that?" I asked, knocking my king over.

"Because people are getting tired of his bullshit. The administration can't protect him forever."

The conversation ended there. I couldn't imagine a thug like Rocky needing protection from anyone. About a year later, gang wars broke out and numerous inmates were getting stabbed. Double D and I still played chess together regularly, but we were a lot more wary.

One day a friend of Dan's, Shorty, got beat up by Rocky over a phone call. Rocky wanted to use a phone Shorty was on, so he just picked up the little guy and threw him to the ground like a rag. Shorty was no coward, but Rocky was twice his size. It was a no-win situation.

Later that same day, Double D took the time to warn me: "Don't come out in the main corridor when they open up tonight. Just stay on the block." But I was too young and curious, unable to imagine that the main corridor could be any more dangerous than it already was. When the evening bell rang, I locked my cell and ventured out, staying close to the guard's station just to play it safe. All seemed normal, except the traffic was extremely light. Too light for a prison of over two thousand men. The main corridor exhibited a dreary glow, like the light of a fading fluorescent lamp.

Suddenly, the corridor became completely empty. A deadly silence gripped the scene. Some feet away, a guard ordered me back to my block as he scanned the corridor in puzzlement. Usually there would be last-minute stragglers loitering about, but now there was not a soul in sight.

As I started for B-Block, I felt a slight breeze. I looked up the corridor to see the auditorium door angled open—inmates were spilling out into the corridor. I was too far away to make out details, but I could tell that a huge mob was quietly filling the back end of the corridor and heading in my direction. It was an eerie, unsettling sight to see hundreds of men rush down a long corridor in utter silence.

Rocky happened to be coming out of the door directly to my right. When he saw the approaching mob, he ran as fast as a man his size could toward A-Block. He banged on the gate, yelling, "Key up! Key up!"

When the mob saw this, they all bolted in unison down the corridor toward him, shouting angrily. The guard on A-Block, instead of retreating to the safety of the guards' station, courageously rushed to Rocky's aid, keyed the convict into his block, and locked the door behind him. Then in some fit of insanity he stood in the center of the corridor, raised his hand, and hollered, "Everybody back to your blocks! That's an order!" But the unstoppable mob ran over him on their way to confront Rocky and his Terminators.

Some men banged on the door to A-Block and screamed, "Key! Key!" Amazingly enough, another guard opened it and let through a stream of men before he realized his folly and slammed the door shut. The rest of the crowd streamed through the door from which Rocky had emerged moments earlier.

Leading the pack were Double D and Shorty. When he saw me watching in amazement from the corridor, Dan waved me away. His mob then disappeared into the dark doorway until all of them had emptied out of the main corridor. All that was left were me and the trampled guard still lying on the floor. Quickly guards hurried out of their station to drag their co-worker to safety. I myself rushed to the B-Block door and was lucky enough to be let in.

Soon the mob returned to occupy the corridor, hollering in triumph. This wasn't the Battle of Lexington or the Boston Tea Party, but the consequences were just as profound for Graterford. No one was killed in this bloodless coup, but things changed rapidly. Rocky, the Terminator's leader, was transferred out of the prison that night. The next day, a number of his gang members were stabbed in separate incidents. Many of the others took self-lockup.

From that day forward, no one gang dominated at Graterford. If Double D's story was true, then the administration had lost its balance of power. Soon whole gangs of cell thieves were being stabbed and beaten. Just as these gangs had once made the administration superfluous, the collective will of the inmate population had now made the gangs superfluous.

Hence, the "Kingdom of Inmates" was born. Its new offensive curtailed much of the stealing that the administration had been unable to control. A collective conscience had risen among the inmates, as Graterford evolved from a ragtag nation of independent tribal gangs into a unified conglomerate of collective and competing interests. It was only a matter of time before the new kingdom would begin to test its boundaries by challenging the power of the prison administration.

10

A Kingdom Remembered

In retrospect, it was primarily the inability of Graterford's guards to ensure inmates' safety that brought about the demise of their control over their own prison. By the mid-1980s, things had changed with overcrowding and the influx of new prison subcultures. Administrators could not hire new guards fast enough to keep pace with the flood of inmates, so the practice of overtime was employed.

The overexposure of tired, irritable, overworked, and sometimes inexperienced and antagonistic guards to the already violent population created an inconsistent and unpredictable prison environment, especially because guards knew much less about what inmates were thinking and vice versa. When things got so bad that inmates couldn't even commit themselves to protective custody, the population knew it had to fend for itself. The only thing guards could do for inmates now was to keep them locked in their cells.

Because of this, the population developed its own unwritten "Inmate Code of Conduct," which stood apart from the prison administration's rules and regulations. The code went something like this: "Don't gamble, don't mess with drugs, don't mess with homosexuals, don't steal, don't borrow or lend, and you might survive."

By itself, this simple rule would never have worked unless something tangible and powerful prevented the inmates from killing each other and forced them to abide by it. That something was the flourishing underground economy. The black market of goods and services had grown so much as a result of overcrowding and failed security that a stable class of merchants and consumers had established itself within the prison population.

The swag man who sold me and others his sandwiches became my friend. But if it hadn't been so easy and profitable to steal from the kitchen, he probably would have ended up stealing from me. The more he provided his clandestine services, the more he created a demand, which in turn ensured him a steady income that was far less risky than breaking into another man's cell. Every inmate in general population was either a buyer or a seller. It was now to everyone's benefit to abide by the Inmate Code of Conduct, so that the economic heart of the Inmate Kingdom could continue to beat.

The only threat to this economic stability, then, became the guards. Because they were no longer the mainstays of stability or providers of protection, their petty rules, shake-downs, and confiscations served only as an irritating nuisance that hindered the inmate population's new economic order. The Kingdom of Inmates had no choice but to challenge the authority of the guards to discourage their interference with the socioeconomic balance.

It is difficult to determine exactly when Graterford's guards yielded their authority to their charges, but one significant turning point took place on Super Bowl Sunday of 1983. An inmate left the C-Block dining room and headed for his cell, openly carrying a paper plate piled high with the usual Sunday chicken dinner and all its trimmings. It was his intention not to let his favorite meal interfere with his watching the Super Bowl on the TV in his cell. Posted everywhere around him were signs dictating, "NO FOOD IS TO LEAVE THE DINING ROOM."

While violations of this rule were commonplace, the usual practice was to hide one's food before leaving the dining hall. To accommodate this minimal demand for obedience, most inmates smuggled out food in anything from trash-bag liners to empty potato-chip bags, often stashed in the split lining of one's institutional prison coat. Guards never searched for food, and no harm was done.

But on this particular day, this inmate had decided to blatantly ignore convention. As was expected, a guard saw him with the food plate, followed him to his cell, and ordered him either to eat his food in the dining hall or throw it out. Considering the circumstances, this was a reasonable request.

The inmate told the guard in no uncertain terms that he planned to eat his Super Bowl meal in the comfort of his cell and there was nothing he could do about it. The guard, frustrated by this display of disrespect, grabbed the plate of food out of the man's hands.

What ensued became known as the Super Bowl Sunday Chicken Riot. Because C-Block housed many winemakers and this was a big sports day, a good number of the block's four hundred occupants were drunk on "pruno," or prison hootch. When they saw this inmate's fight with the guard, everybody decided it was time to show the staff who was boss. Every inmate related to the incident as if the guard had tried to take away something of *his.* The chicken was more than just food—it represented each man's hustle, and its confiscation challenged everyone's livelihood.

Dozens of men swarmed to the aid of the inmate and beat the guard. Dozens more mobbed the dining room to defiantly take chicken dinners back to their cells. In quick order, every guard on the block was assaulted and some were even locked in cells.

Notably, the inmates attacked only guards and not each other. Not a single inmate was hurt in the uprising, which made this event uniquely different from other prison riots. If anything, the inmates actually joined together with a coherent plan. Some seized a guard's radio transmitter and called for reinforcements, while others armed with sticks and clubs waited in ambush by the block's main entrance. When a dozen or so guards rushed into the block, inmates fell upon them like swashbuckling pirates and quickly subdued them. Then they locked their new victims into cells.

What happened next was the most convincing proof that a kingdom had arisen. The inmates abused and humiliated the guards—but they didn't seriously injure any of them. Once they were satisfied, they simply opened the main door to C-Block and allowed other guards to tend to their fallen comrades, just so they could see what might one day await them. Some inmates even assisted the nursing staff in tending to the wounds of guards they had attacked only moments before. There were no demands for better conditions, amnesty, media, the superintendent, or anything else.

And that was the end of the Super Bowl Sunday Chicken Riot. Most of the inmates simply returned to their cells to watch the Super Bowl game, drink jailhouse wine, and eat chicken. Nothing else happened for the rest of the day. At the 5:00 pm count, everyone locked up in their cells as usual. It wasn't until then that guards quietly gathered the rebellious inmates from their cells and escorted them to the Hole.

By then it was too late. The point had been made. Inmates had joined together to defeat the guards fair and square. The interests of the inmate population had been advanced and defended, thus ensuring the livelihood of each and every man in the triumphant Kingdom of Inmates. To this day, Graterford is still the most violent prison in the state system. It now houses over four thousand men and is home to the most politically active inmate population in Pennsylvania.

It was a hot summer day, a Saturday, a time for recreation. Most of the inmates were wearing sweat suits, sweat shirts, or ragtag gym clothes homemade from scraps of stolen cloth. Many of them chose to spend all their recreation time on the block, most of them serious gamblers or avoiding the sun or avoiding a fight.

The gamblers were the easiest to spot because they always played cards on the most private picnic tables in the deepest interior. To a man, they slumped low in their seats, ready at a moment's notice to reach for their weapons. These weapons were usually hidden somewhere below the table, waiting for someone to be caught cheating or prematurely grabbing another man's money. Most other block loungers just milled around, talking, smoking, or drinking coffee as if they were somewhere other than in a maximum security prison.

I had just returned to my cell to change into state whites for my infirmary job. To me, the only difference between hard labor and imposed idleness is the change in a man's appearance. In the end, both will break a man's spirit as surely as his sentence will make him older.

As I left my cell, I heard a distant commotion from the upper range. Hearing it too, the table gamblers slumped a little deeper in their seats, easing closer to their weapons, their eyes never leaving their cards.

Soon I could make out an inmate called Hammerhead Fred running toward me down the narrow walkway of the tier above, with guards in hot pursuit. He was carrying a five-gallon plastic bag, the kind used to dispense milk from a cafeteria cooler with a rubber nipple on one end. But this one was filled with homemade jailhouse liquor called hootch.

As he ran the length of a football field, Hammerhead lifted the bag over his head and forced the booze to flow into his open mouth. Much of it poured onto his face and chest, glazing his protruding forehead and staining his dirty clothes. The heavy bootlegged load was slowing him down, and the pursuing guards were gaining on him.

The whole cellblock was in an uproar, every man cheering him on. "Go Hammerhead! Fuck those hacks! Drink that wine! Don't give it up! Hammerhead! Hammerhead! Hammerhead!"

Just as the lead guard caught up to Hammerhead, an inmate suddenly stepped out of his cell and "accidentally" collided with the guard. The two fell down, and the other guards toppled over them in Keystone Kops fashion.

This gave Hammerhead enough time to take an extra long swallow of hootch. Then he jumped off the second-story walkway and landed upright on a tabletop below. Amazingly, he managed to hold onto his five-gallon bag. His legs spread boldly across the table, Hammerhead guzzled more wine until he had had his fill. Then he hurled the container at the frenzied crowd around him, beat his chest, and gave a savage victory cry.

The crowd screamed, hollered, and beat their chests as they drank from the contraband container, passing it from man to man in a victory-sharing ritual. Finally, the guards got themselves together enough to force Hammerhead down from the table. The inmates booed and hissed as they escorted Hammerhead away, no doubt to a waiting cell in the Hole.

But Hammerhead couldn't have cared less because he was too drunk to feel any pain and more important because today was his last day in captivity. He had served all ten years of his sentence, and he owed no parole time or probation. He was out tomorrow, free and clear.

This was how Hammerhead wanted to be remembered and how he would always be remembered. This is also how I have always remembered Graterford and its Kingdom of Inmates, since the day I myself said goodbye and good riddance to its wretched concrete walls.

11

Battle in the Big House

I didn't know it, but I'd never been in a Big House until I'd arrived at Western Penitentiary, originally built in 1827 and then converted into a Big House between 1878 and 1892. Like most other people, I'd thought Big House was a euphemism for prison, never suspecting it was actually prison slang for a particular design of prison, one marked by mammoth, menacing walls and an empty but rigid daily routine. I also never suspected that one day, I would arrive at the Big House, an exile as a result of violence at Graterford finally coming around to me.

It was Summer 1986, and as usual I had reported to my cell in Graterford for the final 9:30 pm count. As was the practice, a bell sounded to announce count while all four hundred cell doors on the block were levered open to allow block officers to manually lock each inmate in his cell. (In more modern prisons, especially super-max prisons, this and many other activities related to prison management and movement are automated.) This was a tedious and frustrating chore as hundreds of raucous inmates reluctantly returned to their cells to be locked in for the night. Once the count bell was sounded, it took block officers at least twenty minutes to lock everyone in their cells. Because my cell was deep in the interior of the block, my door remained unlocked for at least ten minutes until a prison guard eventually locked me in.

I was seated on the edge of my bed, waiting for the guard's arrival, when suddenly an inmate pulled my cell door open, rushed in toward me, and threw the contents of a large bowl at my face. The stranger's bowl was filled with a sticky, gooey substance that proved to be a mixture of caustic acids, bleach, ammonia, oatmeal, and glue, designed to adhere to flesh so that the acids could inflict maximum pain and permanent chemical burns. My face and eyes were targets of the flesh-eating mud, which could burn and blind me into defenselessness.

Luckily, things didn't turn out the way my attacker had planned. Quick reflexes, honed by years of captivity, allowed me to turn my face away in time for the acid to strike only the top of my head. Made too thick, the acid clung to my thick, curly hair and did not seep into my scalp or ooze down to my face very quickly. Instead, when I flicked my head to face my attacker, much of the clumpy acid fell from my head, leaving only a stubborn patch still sticking to my hair. Eventually, a small amount did finally drip down to my left eye, which I had closed in time to protect my eyeball.

With one good eye, I jumped up from my bed and charged head on into the man who had tried to blind me. I could feel the acid beginning to burn my skin, and I knew I was in a fight for my life. Because I was bigger and heavier than my attacker, our collision bounced him back. It was evident from his expression that he had not expected me to resist. This element of surprise gave me a momentary but critical advantage.

My primary objective was to prevent the attacker from using a shank that I was certain he possessed. I hoped to accomplish this by muscling him out of my cell and into the tier where friends or prison guards might come to my aid. My plan failed when our collision drove him against a wall rather than out the door. Fearing my attacker had cohorts to assist him, I instantly executed Plan B: I pulled my door locked. Now it was a fair man-to-man fight with me possessing the dual advantages of momentum and home turf. One-eyed and scared, I fought for my life.

We fought for the longest ten minutes of my life, during which time I threw at the trapped and armed attacker (he did have a shank) my TV, radio, and everything else I could get my hands on. Finally, I overpowered and disarmed him, pinning both his arms against the floor with my knees. This allowed me one free hand, which I used to stick my thumb into one of his eyes. The man, still resisting, was calling for someone's help, and I could hear somebody pounding on my door, trying to get in.

Now, I had a decision to make: What do I do to the man who had just tried to blind and maybe even kill me? Still thinking rationally, I decided it was fairest and safest to subdue him using the goo, the chemical blob with which he planned to disable me. So, with my free hand, I grabbed a handful of muddy acid, still clinging to the top of my head, and spread it generously on the attacker's face. The man immediately started to scream and demand I get off of him because I was hurting him. Me hurting him! The sheer nerve of his demand so angered me that I quieted him by shoving some of his acid paste into his own mouth.

Guards finally arrived to take the screaming and spitting intruder out of my cell. Meanwhile, I was locked in my cell with my left eye swollen shut. During the fight I felt nothing, but now, in its aftermath, it felt like my face, head, and eye were on fire. So I immediately diluted the acid's potency by washing my face with water from my sink. I couldn't open my eye, so I couldn't tell if it was damaged. About an hour later I was taken to the infirmary, where nurses flushed out my eye with warm water. But the swelling didn't go down, and I still couldn't open my eye. It would take a nervous two weeks before I learned that I could still see through both eyes.

From the infirmary, I was taken to solitary confinement, where I remained for several months while prison officials investigated the incident and decided what actions needed to be taken. One month into my isolation, the superintendent came to visit. We were well-acquainted and shared a very good relationship. He had come to inform me that his boss, the commissioner of corrections, had ordered that I be transferred to another institution. I couldn't believe it. I had been attacked and yet I was the one being transferred!

"Why am I the one being transferred?" I asked.

"Well, let's put it this way. I've never had a problem with you. In fact, I appreciate the lawsuit you filed against the prison because it has gotten me all the money I need to try and fix this place. I never got any money for capital improvement before. Unfortunately, for you, there are some who took your lawsuit more personally, and well, they want you out of here," the superintendent confided.

"What do you mean?" I asked, actually knowing the answer.

"Well, let's just say someone feels you had been treated pretty good over the years, and you have betrayed all the trust and privileges you have received," he answered.

A month before the attack, I had sat for trial in federal court to litigate a conditions of confinement suit that I had filed against Graterford and the Bureau of Prisons (*Hassine v. Jeffes*). In the suit, I asked that double celling in Graterford be stopped until such time as the prison was repaired and staffed to a degree that rendered it legally safe and clean.

Only a few weeks before my attack, I had asked the presiding judge if he would allow me to cross-examine a witness—particularly one of the prison's expert witnesses scheduled to testify about the safe conditions in Graterford. Remarkably, the judge agreed, but he conditioned his approval on the witness being the deputy superintendent of security—the former major of the guards who had been my former employer at Graterford and who had stuck by me during the burger incident. He was still my strongest staff supporter now, years later.

I should have declined the offer, but I desperately needed to feel like a lawyer, if for only a moment. Desperate needs make for bad decisions and so I decided that I could cross-examine the deputy superintendent without offending him or injuring our relationship. So I cross-examined the deputy and, of course, I was wrong.

In November of 1986, the day before a scheduled hearing for the lawsuit, I was transferred from Graterford to Old Western—the Big House, a high-walled monster of a prison. The transfer placed me as far west in Pennsylvania as the Bureau of Prisons could send me: more than six hundred miles away from my family and, coincidentally, outside the jurisdiction of the federal judge deciding my case. This left me too far away for regular family visits and no longer a party in my lawsuit.

My move to the Big House was the first, but certainly not the last, reminder of prison managers' disdain for inmates who publicly complain about prison conditions or treatment. I remained in solitary confinement longer and was transferred farther away than the inmate who attacked me. As measured strictly by punishment, filing a lawsuit challenging the conditions of confinement in a prison is a more serious offense than a violent, unprovoked criminal act meant to blind and possibly kill another man.

In the end, my lawsuit succeeded in delaying double celling in Graterford until after 1988 and required the Department of Corrections to spend more than $45 million in capital improvements to the prison—including the establishment of the State's first privatized prison Mental Health Treatment Unit. It also led to prison managers labeling me a "troublemaker" and over the years transferring me to no less than seven different Pennsylvania State prisons, making me into a kind of living specimen of prison history.

12

Prisons Old, Prisons New

The way I see it, the most significant aspect of the penitentiary system was its innovation of collecting criminals, in a central secure location, for the express purpose of plying them with a specific and uniform process designed to produce a desired end product. In this context, penitentiaries, past and present, are little more than processing plants housing assembly lines that receive inmates, make them into commodities, and then uniformly subject them to various punitive and reformative treatments that are calculated to convert criminals into something more useful or at least less noxious.

In the early nineteenth century, New York's Auburn prison operated under a penal philosophy in stark contrast to the Quakers' approach. What was different was its purpose. The Quakers employed their penitentiary assembly line to deliver isolation and religion for the purpose of producing introspection, which was meant to yield personal reform. Auburn penitentiary's more cynical "congregate system" operated to deliver forced hard labor and brutal physical punishment for the purpose of manufacturing conforming criminals who labored to produce fiscal self-sufficiency for the prison.

A prison assembly line designed to exploit convict labor takes a different form from one designed to promote isolation and introspection. This assembly line needs significantly less square footage of convict living space because an inmate will be forced to labor out of his cell most of the day, only sleeping in the cell at night. Smaller cells are the result. Savings realized from building and maintaining smaller housing units can then be used to maintain a larger prison workforce, dedicated to maximizing the exploitation of unpaid inmate labor, which is to say, slave labor. Consequently, Auburn-style prison structures could be built small and up, rather than long and wide.

A traditional Auburn-style penitentiary consisted of a rectangular containment building, more than five stories high, encasing five tiers of very small cells (three and a half by seven feet), each tier of cells stacked one on top of the other. Once inside a cell, an inmate could not see other cells or inmates. Such a design is perfectly suited for slave quarters.

Sing Sing, New York's most famous Auburn-type penitentiary, was built on a grand scale. In keeping with its cynical penal philosophy, inmate laborers were pressed into service constructing what would ultimately become their own slave quarters. Sing Sing boasted two giant Auburn-style cellblocks with an equally tall administration building sandwiched between them. For purely aesthetic reasons, the street-facing side of Sing Sing was provided with columns and other stylish design elements that, from a distance, gave the administrative building and two attached cellblocks the appearance of a large, multiwinged mansion, hence the term "Big House." Note that the main house on slave plantations was traditionally called the Big House.

Western Penitentiary's construction in the Big House fashion represented Pennsylvania's surrender of its singular commitment to reform and the adoption of the less enlightened prison purpose of conformity in service of fiscal self-sufficiency. Its two cellblocks were of Auburn style and built in succession with the first (North Block), containing five tiers of 128 cells (six feet wide by six feet deep) per tier. When North Block was finally occupied by inmates, the cells proved to be too small for human habitation. (The average size of prisoners had grown over the preceding century; so too, perhaps, had expectations about what constituted a decent penal living arrangement.) Therefore, the second cellblock (South Block) was redesigned to contain 100 cells (seven feet wide by eight feet deep) in each of its five tiers.

When I entered the Big House, I had no awareness that I was to live in what was intended to be slave quarters. Nevertheless, I felt as alone as I ever had before as I walked along the narrow corridor that separated the containing structure from the interior five tiers of cells, on my way to a tiny cell on North Block. Instead of fear, I felt anger and frustration fueled by loss: I longed to return to Graterford, the physical and emotional home of my family and support. Looking back, I see now that my separation anxiety caused me to romanticize Graterford's violence and uncertainty while disdaining the relative calm I intuitively sensed in the Big House. It seems that Graterford, inch for inch the most life-threatening real estate in Pennsylvania, had somehow conditioned me into a violence and fear addict, accustomed to life on red alert.

Western had its own distinctive problems, largely because of the fact that it was always dark and gloomy, much as one would expect from a prison built to house inmates slated for slave labor. Light fixtures were dated and provided shadowy and uneven lighting. Poor lighting made anything requiring vision difficult and uncertain. It was hard to read or write in my cell. The walkways on the block and outdoors, leading to other buildings behind the wall, were shadowy and scary, like walking at night on a poorly lit street in a rundown neighborhood.

The lighting made it difficult, most of the time, to see or identify people or things near me. Blind spots, created by poor lighting, abounded on and off the blocks. This permitted many "war zones" where anything could and often did happen. Danger was hidden not only around every corner but also in plain view, in the open.

The darkness at Western left me apathetic about myself and my safety. I felt lost and at loose ends. I realize now that I had been experiencing depression from separation anxiety and prison conditions. In my case, depression translated into a compulsive animosity and a desire to get even. It's sad to think that by merely providing adequate lighting, Western could have saved prison managers and me a whole lot of unnecessary problems.

This darkness affected prison staff as well, making them feel frightened and vulnerable. Staff's response to unavoidable blind spots is often very much like that of the inmates; they act tough and violent to reduce the risk of being jumped in a dark alley. In Western, this meant that staff did not enforce rules as much as they made certain that they were safe from harm. To enhance their safety, prison staff allowed inmates to attack and victimize each other. Many of us believed that staff sometimes encouraged inmates to prey on one another. Why? Because if violent predators had enough vulnerable inmates to prey on, they would not need to victimize staff.

Allowing, if not encouraging, inmate violence to flourish was not simply an unintended response to prison violence but an unwritten, well-established, and practiced policy of prison staff. Given prison design and staffing limitations, there really was no other way for staff to effectively protect themselves from Western's ever-present blind spots. So if they couldn't stop violence, all that was left to do was to direct it toward someone else. In this case, that someone else was me and all the other inmates.

In a sense, I have lived prison history. First I landed in Holmesburg Prison, one of the oldest and most dangerous county prisons in the nation. Then I was moved to Graterford, a 1934 version of a super-max prison. Next I landed in Western, a century-old prison that marked Pennsylvania's departure from a correction-based penal system. In 1998, I was transferred to SCI-Albion, which had been newly constructed in 1994. Albion boasts of state-of-the-art technology and design and operates under newly minted notions of the nature and purpose of adult corrections. What an eerie feeling it was to enter Albion, having just been plucked from prison-past and suddenly planted in some futuristic prison world.

The order in which I was submerged into my new prison habitats provided me with a historic overview of the various prison models. This intimate contact with prison-past and then prison-present left me able to discern the structural and operational distinctions between the earliest and newest incarceration systems. So, despite the obscuring mist of evolutionary change, I can clearly identify the elements that control the scope, nature, and consequences of contemporary prison management models.

My insight has little to do with intellectual ability. You see, all existing prison systems are nothing more than extensions of an entrenched originating prison bureaucracy. Therefore, the potential for change in any prison system is limited by the inherent nature of its founding bureaucracy. And, despite popular belief, contemporary prisons are not new institutions rising atop the ashes of discarded older ones. Actually, they are merely the new growth of a maturing but still operating originating bureaucracy.

Despite dissimilar design and appearance, super-modern Albion is structurally and operationally a composite of Holmesburg's, Graterford's, and Western's prison management systems and models, but with a new coat of paint. For this reason, understanding the nature and consequences of contemporary prison models requires a careful examination and evaluation of their past originating penal system. In terms of evolution, a prison's past is also its future.

SCI-Albion was conceived and eventually constructed following the convergence of tumultuous events that occurred in Pennsylvania in 1989. Early in that year, the conditions of confinement suit that I had filed against Western Penitentiary was won. Then severe overcrowding led to prison riots in SCI-Rockview and SCI-Huntington. Finally, a four-day-long prison and hostage takeover completely destroyed more than 50 percent of SCI-Camp Hill.

Moved to action by the prison riots of 1989, the legal team, which had successfully litigated the conditions of confinement suit against Western, filed a conditions-of-confinement suit against all of Pennsylvania's adult corrections facilities. The lawsuit was resolved with a consent decree in which the Department of Corrections agreed, among other things, to build six new one-thousand-cell, state-of-the-art prisons.

In 1990, the governor of Pennsylvania appointed a new commissioner of corrections, Dr. Joseph D. Lehman (later commissioner of corrections for Washington State), to oversee reforms to the state's overcrowded and riot-torn prison system and to negotiate and enforce the consent decree. Between 1994 and 1995, SCI-Albion and five other identical one-thousand-cell, prototypical prisons came online in accordance with the consent decree. Commissioner Lehman made certain that the new prisons (six in all) were designed and constructed to accommodate an active inmate rehabilitation model. To me, after having been stuck in Pennsylvania's prison past for almost two decades, the result was breathtaking.

Like most other modern prisons, Albion is secured by a thirty-foot-high, stainless-steel mesh perimeter fence topped with thick curls of stainless-steel razor wire. Therefore, I was welcomed to Albion by the wide if cold grin of its glittering silver-on-silver woven metal fence topped with a tinsel-like razor wire. The transparent fence artistically framed and highlighted the prison scenery, which was clearly visible through its mesh. And instead of being scared and intimidated, as I had been when I first entered Holmesburg, Graterford, or Western, I remember feeling curious and even excited about exploring the beckoning prison I was able to spy through the pretty perimeter fence.

Albion was an ocean of plush green fields of grass with handsome geometric outcroppings of earth-toned brick buildings of various shapes and sizes. The buildings were generously spaced so that the deep green of the grass, the proportionate lines of the buildings, and the surrounding cerulean blue of the sky combined to create an eye-pleasing and harmonious vision of tranquility that evoked safety and relaxation.

All of Albion's buildings are climate-controlled, well-lit, spotlessly clean, and color coordinated. There are security cameras everywhere and blind spots nowhere. There are eight separate general population housing units of only 128 cells each, three separate dining halls, and two huge recreation yards.

Each housing unit has shower stalls, laundry facilities, a spacious day room (with cushioned chairs), two TV rooms, and large windowed cells. Each recreation yard has a paved quarter-mile running track, basketball courts, a baseball diamond, and lots of green grassy landscape. There is also a large gym complex with a full indoor basketball court, two weight-lifting rooms (with free weights, treadmills, and universal machines), a barber shop, classrooms, and administrative offices.

There is as well a large education complex with classrooms, conference rooms, administrative offices, and vocational training rooms. Many of the rooms have banks of desktop computers for student use. There is a separate psychology department with individual counselor's offices and group meeting rooms. And there is a spacious interfaith chapel staffed by three full-time chaplains.

To understand day-to-day life in a contemporary prison like Albion, consider this typical day in my life:

6:00 am

A very loud bell sounds, the lights in my cell turn on automatically, and a loudspeaker announces: "Count time. All inmates stand for count." My cellmate and I get out of bed, stand by the cell door, and wait for two prison guards to pass and count us. Once the guards have passed, we make our beds (failure to do so is a misconduct), take turns using the sink and toilet, and prepare for the start of our day.

6:30–7:00 am

The loudspeaker announces: "Breakfast line. Five on the door." This means that I have five minutes to press a call button located near the threshold of the cell door. This will cause my cell door to be unlocked. My cellmate leaves the cell, locking the door behind him. Then I use the cell's hot tap water to make a cup of instant coffee.

About twenty minutes later, my cellmate returns to the cell from breakfast, and we both remain locked in the cell, awaiting the next line movement. There isn't enough room in the cell for both of us to move around so we each sit or lay on our bunks (I have the bottom bunk) and watch/listen to the news on the TV/radio.

8:00 am

The loudspeaker announces: "Work lines. Education lines." My cellmate and I have five minutes to hit the call button and leave the cell to go to work or school. My cellmate goes to work while I stay in the cell waiting for line movements that will allow me to go through my morning workday routine.

8:15 am

The loudspeaker announces: "Yard out." At this time, I have five minutes to hit the call button to open my cell so that I can go to the yard. Instead, I choose to stay in my cell so later I can take a morning shower. If I go to the yard, I will have to wait until the afternoon to shower and because I work in the afternoon, I will not be able to shower. On workdays, instead of yard, I take a morning shower and then enjoy the luxury and solitude of an empty cell.

9:00 am

The loudspeaker announces: "Half-time move for yard." At this time, men in the yard can return to their cells while men in their cells can go to the yard. The block guard will only open my cell for a five-minute window ("five on the door") during line movements. I hit my call button to get my cell opened so that I can take a shower. Wearing a bathrobe and slippers, I walk the few feet to one of eight stalled showers on the tier. After showering, I return to my cell, get dressed and, because I'm a morning person, I write or read with the radio on; usually I listen to National Public Radio. Inmates are not allowed to use the dayroom in the morning except on weekends. This is to encourage inmates to leave their cells and go to work, school, or the yard.

10:00 am

The loudspeaker announces: "Yard in." Everyone in the yard returns to their cells. I use this opportunity to press my call button so that I can go out of my cell and make a fifteen-minute phone call to my family. (There are four wall-mounted pay phones on the pod.) After the call, I return to my cell.

11:15 am

My cellmate returns from work, and we both wait to go to lunch.

12:00 noon

The loudspeaker announces: "Main line out." We have five minutes to hit the call button and leave the cell for lunch. I join the one-hundred-plus other inmates on the pod who leave their cells to go eat. The design of the block requires us to exit the block in a single column of men. Once out of the unit, the column thickens as inmates pour onto a concrete walkway. I move with the herd along the walkway that leads to a larger perpendicular concrete walkway, extending to my left and right. I turn left at the intersection, along with the herd, being careful not to collide with other men walking in the opposite direction to return to their block after finishing their meal. Blocks are called to meal lines one at a time so that when one block of men is leaving the chow hall, another block of men is called to eat. I eventually enter my assigned cafeteria and go through a food service line, at the end of which I am handed a preplated tray of food and a beverage. I am assigned a seat at a four-man table. I have about seven minutes to eat before the guards order me to finish eating and return to my block.

12:30 pm

I'm back in my cell with my cellmate, a bell sounds, and the loudspeaker announces: "Count time. All inmates stand for count." The lights in my cell are turned on, and my cellmate and I stand up in front of the cell door until two guards go by to count us. I then read or take a nap while waiting for count to clear.

1:00 pm

The loudspeaker announces: "Count is clear."

1:05 pm

The loudspeaker announces: "Work lines. Education lines." We have five minutes to hit the call button. We both go to work. We join the herd of inmates exiting the unit. I walk the maze of concrete walkways to my assigned job in the library.

2:00 pm

At work a loudspeaker announces: "Line movement." Men in the library have five minutes to return to their cells, or they can stay until the next line movement, which will be on the hour. Also, eligible inmates in their cells have five minutes to come to the library. Inmates are allowed to attend the regular library one time per week (per assigned day and time) and the law library twice per week (per approved written request).

3:00 pm

The loudspeaker announces: "Line movement." Inmates in the library have five minutes to return to their blocks or stay until the library closes.

3:15 pm

The loudspeaker announces: "All inmates return to your block." The library is closed, and I have five minutes to return to my cell.

4:00 pm

The loudspeaker announces: "Count time. All inmates stand for count." The lights go on in my cell, and my cellmate and I stand by the cell door until two guards pass to count us. We then return to our bunks to read or watch TV until the evening meal.

4:30 pm

The loudspeaker announces: "Count is clear."

5:00 pm

The loudspeaker announces: "Main line out." My cellmate and I go to chow with the rest of the block. We return to our cell at about 5:20 pm.

6:00 pm

The loudspeaker announces: "Work lines. Education lines." I have five minutes to leave the cell and go to my job assignment. My cellmate has the cell to himself. On weekends I will be able to stay in my cell, use the dayroom, or, in spring and summer months, go to the night yard when yard lines are called.

7:00 pm

The loudspeaker in the library announces: "Line movement." Men in the library have five minutes to return to their cells or stay until the library closes. Eligible men in their cells have five minutes to come to the library.

8:00 pm

The loudspeaker announces: "All inmates return to their block." The library is closed and I return to my cell. I can stay in my cell, play chess in the dayroom, take a shower, or use the phone. I usually use the phone and then play chess.

8:40 pm

The loudspeaker announces: "Lockup for count." I have to return to my cell within the next five minutes.

9:00 pm

The loudspeaker announces: "Count time. All inmates stand for count." The lights in my cell go on, and my cellmate and I stand in front of the cell door until two guards pass to count us.

11:00 pm, 2:00 am, 4:00 am

The "security lights" in my cell go on for nonstanding count. It is a half-light, but it is bright enough to allow me to read. The lights turn off about fifteen minutes later. It interrupts my sleep, even though I wear a towel over my face.

6:00 am

A bell sounds and the loudspeaker announces: "Count time. All inmates stand for count." I get to do everything all over again.

If I had predicted in 1980 that one day I would be housed in a prison that featured the living conditions of Albion, I would have been considered crazy and probably prescribed psychotropic medication. Suffice it to say, strictly in terms of living conditions, being housed in Albion was like living in some on-campus college dormitory.

Rest assured, however, that Albion was no college campus. It was, I learned, a warehouse in disguise. With its large inmate population of twenty-three hundred men, the prison was crowded and uncomfortable. Every inch a very secure and controlled prison, Albion didn't look or feel like an old-fashioned prison because its architecture created an illusion that made its hard and gritty daily grind of prison outwardly appear natural and even benign. This manufactured effect is comparable to that of a store-bought ant farm: The visible order, regularity, and routine of the seemingly content ant colony fails to expose the violence and crushing hopelessness the trapped ants are actually forced to endure. Albion is a crowded and violent place and, in many ways, paradoxically more hopeless and indifferent than any prison that had ever housed me.

13

Modern Ghost Towns

How did Albion, built with such high hopes and good intentions, come to be a failed prison? I believe it is because of the profound disjuncture between its design and operation. Although Commissioner Lehman specifically designed Albion to accommodate a rehabilitation model, Governor Ridge, after forcing Lehman to resign in 1994, went about implementing policies, procedures, and practices directed at undoing or neutralizing many of the prison's reform-minded design elements. In a great twist of irony, Albion—which had been built to correct problems associated with failed attempts to modify Pennsylvania's old punitive prisons into accepting rehabilitation programs and elements—was now having its rehabilitation design modified to accommodate antagonistic punitive programs and elements. In the end, operating Albion in a manner contrary to its design mandates will ensure that prison's failure for the same reasons and in the same way that other correctional structures failed when they tried to accept incompatible reform elements.

Like most contemporary prisons, Albion fragments and meters my time out of the cell to enslave me to line movements that are methodically announced by bells or loudspeakers. A generous estimate of my daily out-of-cell time is less than seven hours. The rest of the time, I am in my cell waiting for count or line movements. My life consists of constantly trying to go or return from somewhere within the five minutes of allowed movement time. This routine of keeping in sync with mass herd movement leaves me too busy to cause a disturbance or plan some mischief.

Controlled line movement erodes efforts at rehabilitation. This is because classroom, chapel, and all other treatment service times are also fragmented into one-hour portions. Thus, when counts are late, which is often the case, the classroom sessions scheduled immediately after count are canceled because they are too short to be of any value. Considering that classrooms are only accessible three and a half hours in the morning, two and a half hours in the afternoon, and two hours in the evening (eight hours total), losing three hours of classroom time because of late counts means losing one third of the available classroom time. Five hours per day of classroom time for an inmate population of twenty-three hundred is simply inadequate.

This erosion of classroom time also discourages inmate enrollment in educational programs and frustrates teachers who, like me, must spend much of their day waiting for count to clear rather than teaching. This frustration results in absenteeism and an increase in social distance between inmates and teachers. In the end, neither students nor teachers feel that participation in educational programs is of any meaningful value.

In 2003, I charted, for a four-month period, classroom cancelations. There were ten one-hour classroom sessions scheduled weekdays between 8:00 am and 8:00 pm. During that time, 43 percent of classroom time was canceled because of teacher absenteeism. This did not take into consideration sessions canceled because of late counts, which I would estimate to be an additional 10 percent. Thus, over this four month period, fully 53 percent of education classes were canceled.

Elevating controlled line movements over treatment programs has resulted in shrinking the availability of such programs in most contemporary prisons. In addition, while Albion's walkways were packed with inmates going to or from the yard, commissary, or chow, classrooms in the overcrowded prison remained eerily empty, silent, and still—a sterile ghost town in the hollow of human activity. The same was true of the large and beautiful interfaith chapel.

In the end, all inmate destinations in a contemporary prison are really to nowhere. This might not make a difference to you, unless you knew that tens of thousands of taxpayer dollars per inmate per year were being used to route inmates around fully staffed but empty classrooms and chapels, to hurry them to nowhere until they are finally hurried out to the free world.

Another consequence of Albion's combination of warehousing and controlled movement is sharply limited inmate social interaction. Inmate masses are continuously segmented into smaller groupings going to separate locations: blocks, yards, dining halls, classrooms, and so forth. Each inmate, his own path to take, must always separate himself from the larger group. This constant fragmentation produces a dominance of self-interest over social integration to a greater extent than prisons like Graterford or Western.

Self-interested inmates are prone to developing antisocial behavior because focusing only on individual concerns erodes one's ability to participate in cohesive or cooperative group activity. In short, Albion was teaching inmates to be selfish. As a consequence, the social distance between inmates was as great as it was between staff and inmates.

Prison security officials actively increase the social distance between inmates to discourage planning of group disturbances or uprisings. To this end, informants are openly recruited and rewarded for providing any information regarding rule infraction—no matter how petty—or past crimes. I saw nothing like this at the other prisons I've lived in. Rewarding and elevating informants attracts many practitioners, which in turn keeps inmates distrustful of each other.

Albion's security department relies almost exclusively on an abundance of informant information. The appetite for such information has resulted in a collection of reports from friends, enemies, and strangers about almost every inmate in the prison. It is the responsibility of individual security officials to decide which reports merit belief and action. Therefore, at any given time, most inmates in Albion are subject to disciplinary action based entirely on a security official's decision to believe an informant's report. Of course, inmates are very aware of this vulnerability—that's the point of it—and this knowledge increases the already wide social distance between inmates.

Case in point: When I arrived at Albion, two security officers, whom I had never met, nevertheless resented me because I had published a book and previously filed conditions-of-confinement suits (they eventually confessed this to me). There is always a percentage of prison staff that are so hostile to inmates that they maliciously target those who dare complain about any aspect of prison conditions.

One day, an inmate was caught with colored pencils, stolen from an art class. The thief noticed my name mentioned in the misconduct report as part of a list of men assigned to that art class session. My name appeared first, so the thief, being an experienced informant, offered to strike a deal: for a reduced sentence, he would implicate me by confessing that I had stolen and then sold him the pencils in exchange for a lenient punishment. Whether the security guards actually directed the thief to make a false statement against me is speculation. What is certain is that based on the thief's statement, I was found guilty of stealing the pencils and threatening the informant for "snitching on me." I was sanctioned to ninety days in the Hole while the thief received only thirty days.

I was in the Hole even though the thief had sworn that I had stolen the pencils at a time when I was on a visit, so his story was demonstrably false. The security officers knew the misconduct hearing system at Albion was entirely dispositional with no truth-finding component. This meant that once I was issued the misconduct, the hearing examiner's purpose was limited to deciding the disposition—that is, the degree of punishment. At the hearing level, innocence is of no consequence. On appeal, prison managers would be left to decide whether to release me.

Gloating, the two guards privately confessed to me that they had decided to use the informant's lies to punish me for being so "arrogant." It was a blessing that they were too lazy to investigate my whereabouts on the day in question or else the informant might have given a statement that I could not have so easily disproved.

On appeal to the superintendent, I was released and fully exonerated after serving twenty days in the Hole. I filed a formal prison complaint and, eventually, a federal lawsuit against the two officers. As a result of my prison complaint, I was reimbursed one hundred dollars for property I lost when I was sent to the Hole. Nothing happened to the security guards because they were just following "procedures." However, they increased their determination to get even with me for complaining about their misbehavior.

Eventually, the two security officers succeeded in having me transferred to a maximum-security prison based on their unsupported claim that I posed a threat to the institution. I spent another ten days in the Hole on my receipt in the super-max facility. No misconduct report had been filed to justify my transfer, so there was nothing for me to appeal. Later, as a result of my federal lawsuit, I received a copy of the "secret" memo used to transfer me. It contained nothing but unsupported allegations of "possible" misconduct.

As a result of my transfer to a super-max prison, my privileges were greatly restricted and my record of adjustment was burdened.

Over the course of three years and soon after a judge decided to allow my federal suit to trial, I was suddenly transferred to a medium-security prison. All my privileges and security levels were reinstated to Albion levels. This is what vindication looks and feels like in contemporary warehouse prisons where—only when necessary—justice is treated as an accommodation you must be willing and able to fight for.

Institutional dependence on informant testimony has turned prisons into training grounds for predatory informants who sell true or false information for benefits, revenge, or just plain fun. The lexicon of informing has been increased to accommodate its refinements: "snitches" are now garden-variety informants who report misconduct that they have personally been made aware of or are actually a part of; "snipers" are informants who carefully watch group or individual activities from a distance to detect misconduct that they can use to rat someone out; and "ear hustlers" are informants who, unnoticed, place themselves within listening distance of groups or individuals to hear about misconduct they can use to do the same.

The fear of being targeted by prison informants has replaced the fear of predatory violence. The anti-social and selfish behavior typified by informants, as well as the mistrust it breeds, travels with a convict when he or she is finally released to the free world. Thus, contemporary ex-cons are totally unprepared for life in a cooperative society where, ideally, anti-social behavior is punished and not rewarded.

Albion is the most comfortable, best designed, most structured, and most attractive prison that I have ever lived in. It looks and feels like it can actually work as a rehabilitative prison, but in fact it is the least effective prison of all. It is a dysfunctional, mean-spirited facility that callously steeps you in despair while it lavishes you with physical comfort.

Albion provides the inmate a sterile environment with faceless bells and voices precisely controlling time and movement for no apparent purpose other than order. It is a place where everyone is suspicious of each other and superficial friendliness is all that can exist. It is a place where perception is the only reality that matters and where induced poverty is used to generate illusory wealth.

In addition, it is a place of great violence but not in the same ways that Graterford or Western were violent. The violence in Albion is subtle and more controlled but just as threatening. It is a violence deeply rooted in hatred for the government, society, and anyone else believed to be responsible for the unfairness, meanness, and despair openly served up to Albion's involuntary residents.

One psychologist, who conducted a long-term offenders group that I participated in, discussed with me her worries about the emergence of a prison gang recently discovered operating in the prison. Albion had only been in operation for five years and had never experienced prison gang activity before.

"I am concerned that gang activity will bring Graterford-style violence into the prison," she confided.

"I don't think you have to worry about that," I speculated.

"What makes you say that? You've been in these older prisons and have seen firsthand the violence that gangs bring into a prison," she responded in surprise.

"This prison is too comfortable and safe for gang violence," I explained.

"What are you saying? You don't believe there is a gang problem? I'm telling you, they have locked up gang members who admit to being in a gang," she insisted.

"There may be a gang here, but it can't be the same as the Graterford or Western gangs," I said.

"What do you mean?" she asked, curiously.

"Well, in Graterford and Western, gangs were created by inmates to protect themselves from other inmates. Gang violence in Graterford reflects the violence that made it necessary. Here, there are no rival gangs and no serious threats of violence between inmates. There are a lot of random rapes and fights but no organized predatory violence that would require inmates to form and join a violent prison gang. This prison is just too safe, comfortable, and over-staffed for that," I clarified.

"So why is there a gang if they aren't going to start trouble?" she asked, challenging my evaluation.

"They are here to make trouble, but if there are no other inmate gangs posing a threat, then the only trouble they can hope to cause is for prison staff which, in my opinion, is the 'gang' those inmate gang members most need protection from," I explained. My point was that Albion was creating its own angry and bitter antagonists who could hope to do nothing in unison except resist the imposed order of the prison.

Certainly, a lone and inept prison gang cannot disturb Albion's order and security. But as prison gangs rise and fall in the soup of Albion's inmate population, evolutionary forces will eventually lead to the development of a gang that specializes in the successful disruption of prison operations.

Confined to a prison, the inevitable consequences of the tension between indifferent prison staff and anti-social prison populations are of no moment to free-world citizens. But the clash between prison order and convict dysfunction will eventually spill into the free world as 95 percent of all convicts are finally returned to an unsuspecting society. And, as anti-social warehouse prison populations continue to grow, more and more of their convicts will spill into the free world to spread their learned fondness for disorder, not as members of prison gangs but as agents of crime waves or domestic terrorism challenging the peace and order of our nation.

To fully grasp the ineffectiveness of contemporary warehouse prisons, consider this. When I was first incarcerated in Graterford, the population of Pennsylvania stood at about twelve million. There were eight state prisons and about eight thousand state inmates. The annual prison budget was well below $100 million. Also, keep in mind that Pennsylvania's prison system is purely punitive in that it does not offer good time, earned time, or any other kind of time credit for good behavior. If a convict receives a five- to ten-year prison sentence, he or she will have to serve at least five years. Consequently, Pennsylvania inmates serve more time in prison than any other inmates in the nation.

Now, let's look at Pennsylvania today. The state's population still stands at about twelve million, so the same taxpayer base that supported the prison system in 1980 is supporting it today. However, there are now almost thirty state prisons with 45,000 inmates, and it cost $1.3 billion this year to fund the prison system.

What did taxpayers get for the five-fold increase in inmate population, fourteen-fold increase in prison budgets, and more than three-fold increase in the number of prisons? They have gained an ever-expanding prison system that continues to grow at a rate much greater than the state's civilian population and a recidivism rate that is higher now than it was in 1980 when there was only a fraction of the inmates and prisons in Pennsylvania. Most important, the citizens of Pennsylvania have received no significant decrease in the overall crime rate. If anything, the Pennsylvania experience reveals that the more a state allows prisons to grow and drift away from attempting to rehabilitate inmates, the more crime rates and the need for prisons will continue to grow.

14

The Runaway Train

Overcrowding is the harbinger of cataclysmic change in our nation's prison system. That change is so profound that it is transforming the very structure and operation of the entire system, not just individual prisons. On the one hand, it is giving birth to a renegade bureaucracy obsessed with maintaining its own uncertain existence in the struggle to retain control over the penal system. On the other hand, it is creating a terrified population of inmates who have lost all sense of security and live like "moment dwellers" with no thought of the future.

To better understand the nature and extent of this transformation, consider the analogy of a runaway train. Imagine you're a passenger on a train. As you travel along, you sense that your train is moving faster than usual. This does not alarm you, but you stop reading your newspaper, take a look at your watch, and then peer out a window. You notice the countryside whizzing past you at an increasing rate. Suddenly you see the train speed past the station where you were supposed to get off.

Now you are alarmed. But a voice over the loudspeaker apologizes for the inconvenience, assures everyone that everything is under control, and promises the train will stop at the next station. The train continues to accelerate.

Soon, the train hurtles past yet another station. You begin to realize that something is seriously wrong. You try to find a conductor or anyone in authority, but you get caught in a crush of passengers who have decided to do the same thing. Again you hear the loudspeaker voice, but because of all the confusion you can't make out what it is saying. In any event, you no longer trust any announcements. The train plunges forward out of control, faster and faster.

The crowd, the uncertainty, and the noise cause panic. It is at this point that the train has been transformed from a vehicle of mass transit to a machine that spreads pandemonium among passengers, who now face an uncertain future.

As panic and confusion rise, desperation sets in. No one cares anymore about their jobs, their schedules, or their futures. Everyone is thinking about right now and how they are going to survive this madness. Every human intuition has surrendered to the primitive instincts of "survival of the fittest." The passengers are no longer passengers, and the train is no longer a train.

Now imagine that you are the train engineer. You were the first to realize the train's acceleration problem. Because you are a trained expert, you felt certain you would be able to fix any mechanical problem. You radio the next station and inform them of the problem, and then you pull out your repair manual and go about trying to fix the engine. But the train continues to accelerate and refuses to respond to any of your efforts. At this point you begin to worry.

As you work feverishly to control the train, you hear passengers banging on your engineer's door. The frustration of your failed efforts, the loud din of the uncooperative engine, and the panicking cries of passengers combine to unnerve you. You angrily take a moment to bark over the loudspeaker, "Everything is under control—please remain in your seats." But the screams and banging intensify as the train continues to accelerate beyond your control. You need help but you know you're not going to get any.

Despite your desperate and futile efforts, you realize that the longer you fail to slow your train, the more problems you'll be forced to fix. Weaknesses in design and construction of the train have caused additional mechanical failures. You find yourself reacting to a multitude of new emergencies that give you little or no opportunity to address the original problem. You know that unless this acceleration is stopped, collision or derailment is imminent.

At this point, you are no longer a trained professional concerned only with train schedules and engine maintenance. You have become a reactionary crisis-control manager who no longer cares where the train is headed. Your main goal now is to avert a catastrophe, and you have to keep those hysterical passengers from interfering with what you're trying to do. Meanwhile, the train races faster and faster.

Now imagine that you are a commuter on a train station platform. All of a sudden you see a train speed past you. You catch a glimpse of passengers banging on the passing windows. You notice that their faces show hysteria and that some of them are holding up signs, which you can't make out because the train is out of control, a runaway.

What you have seen causes you some fear and anxiety until you hear an authoritative voice over a loudspeaker apologizing for the inconvenience and announcing that everything is well under control. You are instructed to wait calmly until your train arrives. Although a bit perplexed, you are at least relieved that *you* will be able to reach your destination on time and in one piece.

But what if that train eventually grows so large that it never passes you by but instead the cars keep coming, one after another, day after day, week after week, month after month, year after year, leaving you standing on the platform with nowhere to go? Imagine new passenger cars, some converted into luxury units. Each car is still crowded but, from the outside, some of the cars look comfortable and spacious with reflective glass windows, adding a contemporary touch. And still they keep coming, a continuous chain of captive passengers.

You live in a free society, you like to think, but this train blocks your view. And when you stand back for a moment, you see that the train now looks like a wall. And that wall, you realize, is a dividing line between those on the "right" and the "wrong" side of the tracks—the haves and have nots, the contented and the discontented. There is you and there is me; there are the "free" and the "unfree."

I am one of those hysterical passengers on the runaway train, and this book is a sign that I'm waving at my window, hoping against hope that someone outside the train can read it and get help to us before a catastrophe destroys us all. Prison administrators are the frantic engineers trying to keep me and the other hysterical passengers out of their way while they work to bring the runaway train back under control.

And you, my readers, are the people standing in the station as we tear by. You live in a normal world with all of its normal worries, such as whether your train will be on time or whether you will be late for work. A brief glimpse of our frantic faces may disturb your normal world for a moment. Will you assume that everything is really all right and go back to reading your newspapers? Or will you to try to get help to those passengers who, in the final analysis, are fellow human beings on the train of life?

15

Stories from the Inside

Victor Hassine felt strongly that his fiction allowed him to explore and expose aspects of the interior, private experience of prison life in ways that his nonfiction observations did not. Through short stories about an insidious, lurking beast that left inmates paralyzed by fear ("The Beast"), a prison wall marred by the blood and tears of prisoners past ("The Crying Wall"), and a librarian whose unconditional acceptance of a seemingly monstrous inmate inspired his reform ("The Prison Librarian", co-authored with Sonia Tabriz), Hassine captures the intimate details of his underground world. These stories, Hassine believed, are fiction true to prison life, offering invaluable insights into the human experience of imprisonment.

"THE BEAST," BY VICTOR HASSINE

Danger stalked the prison forcing its inhabitants to live in a state of fear. Fear was so pervasive it became more than just a feeling—it became the Beast that ruled the compound, the Beast all men dreaded but never saw, the Beast that was always just a moment away, lurking in shadows.

What the Beast let live, it altered, leaving its mark on every man, woman, and child who dared enter its domain. Everyone tried to avoid this predator, despite the hopelessness of trying to avoid something they could not see. Then there were those who believed the Beast possessed the power to change its form and become anything or anyone at any time. Those who thought the Beast had human form, disassociated themselves from all of humanity, suspecting anyone and hence everyone of being the Beast. Like lone wolves, these frightened men walked the prison compound, cowering in anticipation of impending attack.

Some men suspected the Beast in the food they ate. They changed their diet, eating only fruits, vegetables, and garlic, hoping this would keep the animal away. Finally, there were those who felt that their safety depended on being constantly in the company of a large group of people. Thinking their antagonist would not attack the many, these men were never alone. Instead, they chose to abandon their individuality for the useless shelter of unquestioned conformity under the rule of others.

Then, of course, there was the physical evidence of the Beast that stood as a constant reminder of this creature's awesome might. The multiple layers of slimy fungus lining the walls and ceilings of the shower rooms had the footprints of the Beast. The uninterrupted chatter of loud voices that echoed throughout the prison carried the victory cry of the Beast. Wounds and scars bore the mark of the Beast. And blood everywhere, on the floor, on the walls and on clothing, was scabbed testimony of the Beast's savagery.

The Beast was everywhere in prison, ready to attack the suspecting and unsuspecting alike. It was this pervasive, pernicious foe that gave the prison its deadly character. It was the Beast who made the killers kill and the rapists rape because all men fear each other less than they fear the Beast.

Like everyone else in the prison, Buck knew of the Beast and was frightened by it. Unlike the others, he held an unhealthy curiosity that wanted to see the Beast; to know the face of the creature that threatened his life. He wanted to see the Beast and thereby be less afraid for having seen it or maybe to see it and to die.

Buck was certain Old Head had seen the Beast. He could see it in the old man's tired eyes, in the way the old man would always be looking around. The constant strain of seeking had caused large balloons of flesh to form beneath sunken eyes, which forced him to squint. Buck believed those vigilant eyes were looking for something they had seen before.

Buck never talked about the Beast to Old Head. Buck was worried that Old Head would sense his fear. Showing your fear in prison was the same as showing your ass; if you did, you could count on someone trying to exploit it. So Buck never spoke to his old friend about his fears even though he often wished he had the courage to do so.

Buck decided to walk the long corridor to the yard. Unavoidably, he ran into Silky the 'swag man,' who was trying to sell his nasty but popular bootlegged sandwiches.

"Hi, Buck, I got a real toe-tapper here for ya. I mean this sandwich is hollering and screaming—jumping up and down. Fried eggs, fish, and cheese hot out o' the kitchen. That's what I'm talking about!" pandered the merchant.

Though amused by Silky's salesmanship, Buck knew from painful experience the consequences of eating a "Silky Swag." Nevertheless, listening to the man's hustle made Buck's mouth water and hunger nip at his empty stomach. Buck was certain Silky could sell a hungry lion to a helpless lamb.

"Nah, Silky, I think I'll pass on this one. The last 'toe-tapper' you sold me gave me the runs," responded Buck while rubbing his belly.

"Hey, that wasn't one of my swags. I was selling that stuff for some dude on 'D' block as a favor. I swear I'll never do that again! I'll tell you what I'll do, Buck," persisted Silky. "I'll give you 'two for one on the eye' and if this sandwich ain't a smoker, well, you ain't got to pay me."

Buck began to smile, impressed by this man's drive and determination, yet remembering the churning pain of his stomach when digesting a Silky sandwich. This proved too great an obstacle for Silky's tempting offer to overcome. Then just before Buck could verbally reject the bargain, he heard a commotion behind him. Bumps ran up the back of his neck as blood rushed to every muscle in his body leaving his face pale and cold. The Beast was near.

Silky must have expected the Beast, too, because swags and all, he was gone. Obviously, Silky did not share Buck's need to see the face of the Beast and so it was that only Buck was there to turn around and face the animal.

A crowd of faceless men bubbled around directly in front of Buck in the boiling commotion of a prison dispute. The din of angry voices swelled while the putrid stink of the Beast filled Buck's nostrils. Despite the fear, Buck could not run away like Silky. Buck's curiosity and stupidity kept his feet from moving, and left him standing terrified before the crowd, reluctantly prepared for the attack of the Beast.

As the crowd grew and the noise increased, Buck expected to hear the savage cry of the Beast, but there was no howling. As Buck watched, what resembled a bolt of lightning came thundering down, hitting a man in the center of his chest. Unlike lightning, the silver flash did not just vanish into thin air. The silver streak just rested, lodged in the man's chest until blood turned the silver red. That's when the shank was pulled out of the man's chest and then plunged into his stomach where it was left, horizontal against the force of gravity.

The crowd soon disappeared and the voices were silenced as the corridor emptied more quickly than it had filled. Soon there was no one left in the corridor except one dying man against a wall, who was slowly sliding down to the floor, and Slim, who just stood there watching him die.

The man had his back against a wall, as his hands gripped the bloodied shank still protruding from his stomach. His life oozed out in a rhythmic pulse that marked a path downward to the cold concrete floor. As a gruesome puddle of blood welled up on the lonely walkway, morbid thoughts came over Buck who noted that blood was much darker than he had assumed and smelled as bad as a Silky swag.

The dying man, who was now on the floor, looked up at Buck and feebly tried to say something. While either begging, cursing or praying, the man then reached out his hand to Buck, who was still trying to break free from the grip of immobilizing fear. Spittle and more blood began to trickle down from the man's mouth. Buck became aware that the man was staring at him with glazed lifeless eyes. Buck had seen that look many times before on men who were high on drugs. The familiarity of the expression strengthened Buck's resolve to face the Beast once and for all, to force the thing from his nightmares.

Suddenly the dying man lurched forward with his hands still outstretched. Buck could hear the sound of air escaping from an open throat as the scent of death assaulted him. The man now lay dead at Buck's feet, which finally were able to move and take Buck away from the murder scene.

As Buck hurried down the corridor to the yard, he wondered if anyone could ever get any closer to seeing the Beast he'd seen reflected in the eyes of the dying man. Soon, guards were rushing past him in the direction of the killing. The foul stench of death, which lingered in his nose, was pushed deeper into him in the wake of their passing.

It was a sunny day in the yard and Buck could feel the warmth of the sun upon him. Nervously he lit a cigarette and began to walk the yard, more aware than ever that he could escape nothing in prison.

"Hey, Buck, what about that swag," asked Silky who had spotted him and managed to catch up with him. Silky was more eager than ever to sell his goods, as if the man's death somehow made his putrid sandwiches more palatable and less obscene.

Silky knew a man had died pitilessly a few moments ago. This realization made Buck hate the persistence of the merchant that a short while ago had humored him. Buck did not respond but instead began to walk faster. Silky followed and continued his efforts. Buck stopped and listened to the savage cry of a wild beast that he was certain everyone heard, but if anyone did hear it, they did not act like it. Buck was scared and confused. There was so much he had just seen, yet didn't understand.

"Well how about it, Slim?" asked Silky.

"Look, Silky, I don't want none of your lousy sandwiches. Now leave me alone," demanded an angry Buck.

Silky walked away, looking for another potential customer. Buck continued walking, preferring to be alone with his thoughts. The more Buck reflected on what he had just witnessed, the more he convinced himself the dead man never asked him for help. Halfway round the yard he convinced himself there was nothing more he could have done. On the second lap around the yard, he was sure it was none of his business. By the third lap, Buck had accepted the possibility that he was never there and he began to feel comfort in this denial. The Beast had gone away, and Buck forgot about the reflection he had never seen in the eyes of a man who had never lived to die.

"THE CRYING WALL" BY VICTOR HASSINE

Morning is born and the cell block is still. Most inmates lay low, because they know, once out of bed, some chore awaits them. Despite this, the freshly arrived inmate got down from his bunk and decided to leave his cell and explore the prison. Trying to get used to walking only where permitted, he took the opportunity to watch curiously as other men passed by on the way here and there. He would later realize that they were actually on the way to nowhere.

From this backdrop of tedious convict traffic, the young man picked out a much older convict standing in front of the enormous and impenetrable prison wall. The man had a damp white towel in one hand and a water filled bucket in the other. He was gently, carefully, almost lovingly wiping the dirty, bruised and discolored face of the aging wall.

Wondering why this old man would be taking such good care of a wall that did nothing more than separate him from the free world, the fish ventured over to where the old man labored.

"Tell me, old man," he asked, as he stood watching watery tears stream down the crusty prison wall where the old man gently dabbed with a wet towel, "why you doin' that?"

"Doin' what?" the old man responded, keeping his eyes on his work.

"Cleanin' that damn wall, that's what! You crazy or something?" the younger man asked.

"No, I ain't crazy, young-sta, leas' no more dan you is," the old man said as he continued to caress the wall with his toweled hand.

"Then why you cleanin' something that don't do nothin' but keeps you from goin' home?" the young man asked, becoming angry for the lack of attention. He couldn't believe the old man was paying more attention to the wall than to him! Where was the respect?

The old man slowly dropped his wet towel into the bucket of clean water at his feet. Then he turned to face the young man who had disturbed his labor of love.

"Come here, young-sta. I wants to show ya' somethin'," instructed the old man, extending an arm in invitation. The younger convict hesitated. "What ya' fear'd of young-sta?" chuckled the old man. "I won't hurt ya'. My fightin' days is ovah. Come here now and lets me show ya' dis-here."

The apprehensive young convict finally did as he was asked, and soon he was standing beside the old man.

"Ya' sees dis-here spot?" the old convict asked as he pointed to what looked like a long dark stain that meandered downward and disappeared into the ground. "I cans hear her cryin' all the times.

That's when these here tears get to pourin' down somethin' awfuls sometimes. It jus' wouldn't be right for me nots to wipe them tears offen 'er."

"You've got to be kidding!" answered the astonished youth. "That there ain't nothin' but water stains from the rain and you ain't nothin' but an old fool."

"Now you jus' watch how you talks to me, young-sta. I ain't too old to slap the sass out-ah young punk kid who be coward 'nough to disrespects an old man," the agitated old convict bristled in as angry a tone as a toothless mouth could summon. Then, with a withered and frail hand, the old man grabbed the younger man and pulled him closer to the wall.

"Ya' sees this red spot here?" he asked, pointing to a large ocher stain that scarred the stone wall. "This is where a young boy—'bout your age—got a piece ah steel shoved inside 'em—over nothin'. That there's his blood. And ya sees that there?" he directed, pointing to a collection of depressions that resembled imprints left by fingers that had tried to grip stone. "Them there's finga-prints of another young mans that done got beat to death right where you standin' because of more dumb stuff. And right there," the old man continued, pointing to some round holes in the wall, "is where the police went and shot some mens who was fussin' over how we was bein' treated in here. Four good mens died that day—ain't none of them much older than you—they died over nothin'."

The young man didn't know what to do. He wasn't scared of the old man but, then again, he wasn't sure what a crazy old man was capable of doing, so he just listened as the elderly convict continued to speak.

"When they first builded this here prison, this wall, she was somethin' to looks at, all shiny white and pretty. She was somethin', she was, standin' all tall, proper and proud, but the years ain't been good to 'er. She done got old, tired and dirty. Young mens, like you, don't treat her right no more. Don't cleans 'er or takes care of 'er."

The old man paused for a minute to wipe a tear from his own eye. Meanwhile, the young man still couldn't believe what he was hearing.

"But you want-ah knows what really done 'er in? It weren't old age. Hell, she was builted to lasts forevah. No sir, she can't ever gets old. What broke 'er down was the ugliness she done had to look at all these years. Young mens like you killin' and hurtin' each other over nothin'. Blood, bullets and mens who ain't nothin' more than children beggin' for mercy while other mens kick them and stomps them dead for a pack of smokes or some other triflin' thing. She done seen it all. She seen thousands of mens grow old and dies all alone in this here place as if they was never someone's son or father or friend. She done seen mens take away they's own lives right in fronts of 'er. I thinks that's why she be cryin' all the time, and I can't says I blames 'er. I means, a lady can't sees all that sufferin' and killin' and dyin' and not cries some."

The old man, with weary, moist eyes, his face as battered as the wall, stared hypnotically into the young man's empty face and said, "An' I could never lets no lady cry without least wipin' 'er tears off. No sir! My mama done taught me better than that. This here wall been cryin' a whole lots lately ovah you young bucks comin' here, all strong, wild and mean and doing nothin' more than killin' each other and yah-selves."

The young man could take it no longer, and broke free of the old man's spell. "Old man, you're nothin' but a crazy fool. You're cleanin' a wall that takes your freedom. You should be tryin' to tear it down, not clean the damn thing!" he barked angrily. "I ain't got time to talk to no old fool who don't want to be free," the young man concluded as he turned and walked away in disgust.

The old man just silently stared up at the old prison wall, dipped his hand into the bucket of water and retrieved a wet towel that he slowly twisted damp-dry and continued to wipe the wall clean.

"Don't pays him no mind, missy. He just mad 'cause he knows he dyin'. One day he'll figure it out. He'll learn that lovin' something else 'nough to do what ya' cans to stops it from cryin' is the onlyest way a man can gets hisself free in here. Shhhhh. You hush now and stops that cryin'. He'll learns soon enough, and then we'll all be feelin' a whole lots better."

"THE PRISON LIBRARIAN" BY SONIA TABRIZ & VICTOR HASSINE

You shoulda seen me when I first came into this joint. I was scared and soft, and all I could see was "Sink or Swim" written on every tattoo, uniform, and wall. I decided I had to swim. I didn't want to end up like one of them floaters: weak cons treated like prison debris to be pushed, pulled, and used by anybody for any reason. A lot of fish—newbies—come up floaters.

I ain't proud of what I ended up doing in here to stay right. But like an old convict taught me, I had to do whatever it took to keep cons, guards, and insanity from creeping up behind me and taking away my pride. No sir, prison ain't no place for the weak. A man's got to stay vicious and heartless to swim with the sharks in these treacherous and hungry waters.

I'm not sure why, but that old convict schooled me well. Now I don't worry about anything 'cause I learned how to lurk silently, like a shadow, leaving cons anxious, wondering when I'll strike. The old con could have just as easily drowned me in the black depths of this angry sea, where no one would listen or care about my cries for help. But he didn't. Instead, he took me in and told me this story that I keep remembering; the one I've been telling some newbies, and wanna share with you.

I guess he decided to make me the keeper of his story so that I could pass it along when he moved on, like he did. I ain't ever before been the keeper of anything but trouble and bad luck. But I guess he just took a chance, hoping that there was still something more human than criminal inside of me. God, I hope that old bastard was right.

The story he told me was about a man, born Jack Jones, who was the meanest and most vicious street thug around; a man whose hard life had turned his heart stone cold. Those who knew him said he was a "hell-raiser," a demon who cared little about himself and even less about others. And this joint didn't make him any better. He became even angrier, with nothing to live for. He told everyone that he wanted to maim and kill as many people as he could, so their souls could be as empty, miserable, and dead as his own. So in time, Jack earned a more appropriate title, "Murder and Mayhem," or M&M.

A swift and solid hulk of a man, M&M started his bit with only a five-year sentence for savagely beating some folks whose only offense was to be happier than he was. But, within a few years, his sentence was increased to thirty years—for stabbing fellow convicts who he felt were not as strong, angry, or hateful as they should have been.

Eventually, M&M did stop stabbing people, but not because he had a change of heart or worried about getting more time behind bars. Not at all. It was just that, after years of being terrorized by M&M, cons and prison guards alike had learned to stay as far out of his reach as possible. And that was fine with M&M, because he was eager to do his time and leave prison. Then he could take his mission to the unsuspecting people of the free world who he blamed for his cruel and heartless ways.

It eventually became a custom for passing convicts to shout out questions to M&M—from a safe distance, of course. It was always the same kinds of questions which received the same kinds of answers. But the cons didn't mind, and apparently neither did M&M, because he spared the fearful convicts their lives.

"What's happening, M&M?" cons would ask.

"Murder and mayhem when I get out; that's what's happening," would come a stern response.

"What you so mad about?" would come another question from behind.

" 'Cause I ain't killed nobody today," an angry M&M would reply.

"What you gonna do when you get out?" someone would always ask.

"Make 'em pay," would be the answer, in a deep and deadly growl. And then the questions would start all over again, in an endless cycle of provocation and response.

Now, to the free world, this endless daily routine would seem unbelievable and considered the product of exaggeration. But, as any convict knows, prison is nothing but repetition and redundancy. Everything that a con says or does is something he's said or done a thousand times before. Only way you'll last is to give in to the routine and act cold and tough. Eventually that's all you become, but at least you're still alive. That's what the old con taught me before God answered his prayers and carried him out of this hole: "You gotta find somethin' to keep you from losin' your brains." He escaped this place by telling stories to new fish like me. And M&M? Well, he escaped by reading stories; one in particular, as it happens.

That's right, reading. In a world where most people communicated with their fists, enjoying a good read isn't how you'd expect a guy like M&M to handle his rage. But cracking open a good book was the only thing that didn't incite or provoke Murder & Mayhem to act on his name and crack open a few heads.

Once a week, for exactly two hours—which is all the prison rules allowed—M&M could be found in the small and shelf-bare prison library, sitting alone at a weathered wooden table, quietly turning the pages of a tattered book that he gripped awkwardly with his mighty, oversized hands. At first, other cons in the library would attempt to provoke M&M—like always, from a distance.

"Look who's got a soft side!" Or, "Hey! Is that a tear I see?" But no matter how much they tried, as long as M&M was in that pathetic prison library, he would not respond to any of their questions. It was as if the book he read possessed him, carrying him to a world so distant from his own that the massive, tattooed frame of his body could do nothing more than sit, awaiting the return of the M&M the cons all knew and feared.

The shabby prison library was run by a librarian, Sophia, a petite woman with fine strands of misty brown hair that cascaded down her back and fluttered with every step she took. She would have drawn no special notice if she'd worked in a library on the outs, besides maybe the snickers of young teens. But amidst the windowless gray walls of the prison library and surrounded by large men with faces set hard to make them look tough, such a small and delicate creature seemed as out of place as a warm smile.

It was truly a sight to see, when the kind and innocent librarian would stand near the menacing men as she made her rounds through the library. "Still working on that one? Let me know when you're ready for the next. The county cleared out their duplicates again this month so I have some new books in the back," Sophia would whisper gently, so as to not disturb the others. "I put aside a few mysteries, Nancy Drew I think. You may like them."

And the cons treated her right for the most part, knowing the guards would make their lives hell if they gave her any problems. But even with two guards standing at the library doors counting down minutes, the cons in the library flinched, looking away the first time the librarian approached M&M. They did not want to witness what they thought would be a cruel attack upon the fragile Sophia by a monster who openly detested kindness, as if it were a deadly enemy.

One man called out, ready to warn her, but she didn't hear. The unsuspecting librarian stood alongside the seated M&M, leaned over and said, "Hi! I see you here a lot but you never ask for help. I'm Sophia, the head librarian, and can help you find anything you are looking for. Do you have any topic in particular you're interested in?" Nothing. "Alright, well let me know if something comes to mind. A lot of the guys here like reading mysteries so I grabbed one off the shelf for you. If you like it, I can find you more of the same." Again nothing. M&M didn't even lift his head, intent on making out the oversized words on the colorful page he was so captivated by.

But as she started walking away, she heard a faint "thank you," just barely over a whisper. She knew M&M didn't want the other cons to hear him sound soft, so she kept walking—like she hadn't heard a thing. He appreciated that.

Sophia helped M&M the next few times he visited the library, and from then on, they were regulars. The sight of the two of them together was so astonishing that the small and usually empty prison library soon began to fill with cons who would come to watch the unlikely encounter. Once a week, in a union of opposites, M&M and the librarian would meet to exchange books and discuss which he would like to read next.

"Perhaps you'd like to read some poetry? Here's one, Tales from the Purple Penguin. It's a book of poetry in the form of short stories. Or something about a young boy's childhood in the South?" She would bring over a few books, and with a simple nod or gesture, he would indicate the ones he wished to read. He moved slowly through the text but Sophia didn't want his requested books being torn up or tossed. So she would put them away in the back, labeled with his name: "Jack."

Their encounters were brief, easy, and almost natural, the old convict would tell me, which was entirely unnatural for the prison. She called him Jack, and he was fine with that.

"Hi Jack, how's it coming along? Looks like you put a good dent in that one. Check these out and let me know if you want me to keep them in the back for you."

And he would nod his head, rarely lifting it towards her direction. She would never ask about content, she wouldn't even mention characters or author names. Some cons questioned whether M&M could even read the words inside the books he grasped with such gratitude, and she didn't want to embarrass him if that was in fact true. Unlike the rest, she didn't want to humiliate him or taunt him. The guards would spit in his food and cons would try to rile him up so he'd act out and get sent to the hole. But Sophia treated M&M differently than they did, by treating him the same way she would treat anyone else.

For decades, the cons were disappointed that M&M seemed to have a soft spot for the librarian. It's not that they disliked the librarian, but in a world full of hate and anger, her kindness must have reminded them of all the things they'd been denied for most of their lives: care and respect. She treated them not like cons, but like people. People who mattered. And M&M treated her like a person too; a person who mattered to him, rather than an object of his hatred for a life he found to be unjust. But no one dared to bring this up to him, for once he stepped out of those library doors, darkness returned and M&M was reborn.

Finally, thirty years after he had first arrived at the prison, M&M's sentence was complete and he stood ready, in front of the long corridor that would lead him to freedom. Every con in the joint stood near so they could watch M&M move one slow and heavy step after another, closer to the free world of unsuspecting victims. Decades of incarceration had certainly aged him, but they had in no way diminished his vitality or his rage. And, it was this undying, pent up fury that made M&M as dangerous as he had ever been. It was a frightening scene, as blood-thirsty cons cheered, wondering if M&M would make good on his promises and fulfill his mission with a vengeance shared by the inmates he left behind.

But, moments before M&M was about to reintroduce his rage to the public, Sophia walked out from a side room, stood directly in front of the walking mountain of hate, and stopped him in his tracks. As the story goes, every con stopped cheering to silently watch what they thought would be his first attack on the free world. Instead, what they witnessed was something they would have never expected. The tiny librarian said ever so softly, "Don't forget to read your favorite book, Jack. It heals the soul." He nodded.

Jack now knew it was a sin to kill a mockingbird, and he knew there lived a mockingbird in the heart of every person. But most importantly, Jack knew that prisoners, even the so-called hardened cons, were people too—with hearts housing mockingbirds that longed to break their silence and sing freely.

"Well, that's what happened for real," the old con told me. But as you might imagine, there are many variations to this story, each recalling a different version of the words spoken between the two and what book was given. Some even swore seeing M&M grin humbly, an act of humanity the monster had never before displayed. But, whatever was said or given that day, everyone agrees that when M&M continued down the hallway, there was a new air about him; like something heavy and unwanted had suddenly been lifted from his shoulders. The grudge he held against those he blamed for his misfortunes seemed to fade as his stern march turned into a proud walk. And the glare in his eyes began to reveal a broken soul, anxious to start anew rather than hold on angrily to the past. But despite this noticeable change in the man they had feared for so long, the cons resumed their cheering, spurred on perhaps by hope for themselves, clapping and hollering long after M&M had left the prison.

For weeks, months, and even years, those who remembered M&M eagerly searched newspapers, expecting to read that he had in fact carried out all the murder and mayhem he had spoken of. Never happened. Instead, a decade later, an article appeared in the local paper naming him "Citizen of the Year." It explained that upon leaving prison, Jack Jones had gotten a job, gone to school, and gotten married. With his wife, he had opened a bookstore, Burnt Offerings, which had become a very successful enterprise. The reason for the award, the article revealed, was that Jack Jones had donated money to build a free public library in his old neighborhood. And at the end of every month, when he would clean out his shelves to stock newly released books, Jack would bring by any easy or interesting reads to the prison where Sophia, the librarian, would offer them to the cons—as she had done with him years ago.

His life was changed, Jack explained to the columnist, not by thirty years of incarceration, but by a book he had received and the kind librarian who had given it to him. He wouldn't name the book, but simply stated what it taught him: inside a tough man beats a tender heart.

So this is the story I've been telling the newbies, who walk in here acting all tough but quickly realize they are just as lost as the rest of us. Having become an old con myself over the years, I am finally preparing to take my walk down the long corridor to freedom; but instead of excitement, I feel lonely and scared. You see, like Murder & Mayhem, I too spent most of my time here trying to act hard; waiting for my chance to get back at the happy-go-lucky people on the outs and be free from this prison hell. But in my old age, I have come to realize one thing: taking off the handcuffs doesn't make me a free man. Freedom is about releasing all the anger and hate that got me here in the first place. It's about finding a way to escape the M&M inside me, like Jack Jones did. Writing stories like this one is my inspiration. It's how I leave my past behind. It's how I set my soul free.

DEATH WITHOUT

Closing Reflections on Living and Dying in Prison Today

by Robert Johnson & Sonia Tabriz

Prison is a world more readily defined by what is missing than what is present. Prison is "life without," as any prisoner would tell any civilian willing to listen. Those two words, life without, say a lot. The prisoner is alive, but he lives without most, if not all, of the things that make life worth living. His is a world of deprivation and loss, an empty universe steeped in dread. The prisoner lives without the possessions we use to define ourselves, the comforts we use to distract ourselves, the relations with others we use to sustain ourselves, the sense of safety we need to go about our daily lives, and the hope we need to persevere through the hard times for a better tomorrow.

Variety, the spice of life in the real world, is conspicuously absent in confinement. Daily life in prison offers what one life-sentence inmate called "hypnotic boredom" that casts its numbing spell against a background of "draconian dreariness." The human environment of the prison, he continued, is "stone cold," as if bodies, not persons, lived in those cages we call cells and many prisoners, sadly, call home.[1] Reducing prisoners to the status of bodies stored in bleak human warehouses violates their human dignity. People can and do exist in prisons for long periods of time, even for entire lifetimes, but the price in human suffering is profound, perhaps even incalculable for us who have the luxury of a life beyond the prison's walls.

For most of us, dignity boils down to a sense of our worth as human beings. That sense of worth, in turn, derives from living in environments that are reasonably safe, that allow us to make choices that affect our lives in important ways, and that allow us to connect—or not connect—to other human beings in supportive personal relationships. Prisons, as we have seen, are places where dignity is undermined. They are dangerous environments; they are settings in which prisoners are under the thumb of authorities who do not treat them like fellow human beings; and they are places in which inmates are denied healthy relations with others and sometimes forced into unhealthy if not outright demeaning personal and sexual relations with others (both fellow inmates and staff).

Inmates are the pawns of the prison world; they are the inconsequential commodities whose dignity is sacrificed at will in the name of expediency. Social psychology tells us that people need a modicum of privacy to preserve a sense of themselves as distinct from the surrounding environment.[2] Prisoners have no claim to such privacy. They can be stopped and strip-searched at any time and any place in prison. Anyone can look in their cells, observe them on the toilet, videotape them when they shower, even make them expose their orifices for inspection as if they were cattle. Prisoners are always potentially, if not actually, under the gaze and control of the authorities. Life on these terms proves unbearable for many people, producing widespread depression.[3] For some prisoners, and especially lifers, suicide may be seen as the last act of autonomy open to them, a way to break out of their depression and, in an existential sense, break out of the prisons that have come to define their lives.

In a telling sequence, Hassine compares modern prisons to ant colonies, sometimes called ant farms, of the sort a parent might buy for a child. Unlike ant colonies found in the wild, which have a rough-edged, disorganized quality to them, fabricated ant farms are neatly structured in exacting detail, the ants move in rigid patterns along predetermined routes, and all activities are visible to outside observers. Children can spend hours absorbed in the neat little regimented world that unfolds before their eyes. Like mock ant farms, Hassine tells us that some of our more modern prisons can be clean and well ordered too, but as human habitats, these environments are profoundly sterile and degrading. A sense of self, marked by autonomy, personal security, and relatedness to others, is precluded in this rigid, controlling, artificial world. In even the best penal approximations of an ant farm, in other words, prisoners live like creatures ruled by setting-specific instinct rather than human beings endowed with choice. Perhaps one can live in this dehumanizing way for a time, but for a lifetime? And is the very notion of a "lifetime in prison" a contradiction in terms, if your days are better characterized as an extended existence culminating in an empty death, rather than a meaningful life that might yield a meaningful death?

Lifers experience this dilemma—are they living or merely existing?—in the context of a growing awareness of the awful deaths so common in prison, which loom like bad dreams foreshadowing their futures. Their futures are indeed bleak, as research reveals that "institutional failures resulting in the needless loss of life are occurring in jails and prisons from every region of the country."[4] These chronic failures have given rise to a "quiet brutality of needless suffering and preventable deaths" that is seen as a hidden cost of doing time in prison today.[5] Tragically, prisoners understand all too well that they live in a world in which their suffering doesn't matter, "where it is acceptable that enormous numbers of human beings are warehoused far away from public view,"[6] destined to suffer and die alone.

Long-term prisoners, and especially those serving terms of life without parole, can be expected to experience poor health relative to their cohorts in the free world and to be exposed to chronically inadequate medical care. Health problems escalate dramatically after lifers reach the age of fifty, leading to shortened life expectancies and early and often painful deaths.[7] Describing the deaths of long-termers at Angola, life-sentence prisoner John Corley observed: "They died because years of continuous incarceration sucked the very life from them, slowly, a day at a time, a torment worse than an inquisitional persecution. They died in dark rooms behind locked doors calling for their mamas."[8] Some prisoners are demonized even in death, dying in shackles, in isolation from even the few friends they may have made in prison.[9] All too often, prisoners die "alone, unmourned, a disgrace in the person's own eyes as well as in the eyes of society."[10]

Perhaps, then, it is unsurprising that many lifers turn to suicide. The unbearable monotony and pointlessness of a life lived to its painful and often degrading conclusion in prison may have been too much for Victor Hassine to bear. He had aspirations to a real life. And for many years, he kept hope alive that he would have a chance to live again in the free world. When that chance was not granted, Victor may well have concluded that his life was effectively over, that the purpose he was destined to serve in prison had been achieved. All that was left was the prospect of a dignified death. That death—a death without the cruel insults of prisons, a death on his own terms—took the form of suicide.

This book is the legacy of a life relegated to prison but also of a life that transcended prison. Victor Hassine was no passive victim of fate. He reflected on the experience of confinement, gave that experience meaning, and conveyed that meaning to others. What we do with that knowledge is up to us. Victor has done his job. Now we must do ours—whether it is simply to better understand the prison world he described for us in such telling detail, or perhaps more ambitiously, to work to reform our penal institutions, bringing a life-sustaining hope to their many captives.

We end this book on the inspirational words of the Hassine family, who knew him better than anyone, and hope that their words and this book will keep Victor's memory alive:

> Victor was a positive thinker. Of course, during the 25 years confined to the four walls of his prison cell, he had many dark moments and crises in confidence. But always, he got through it all by thinking positively. He would get out of prison one day. He would resume his life. Get married. Have a family. Meanwhile, Victor would make the most of a horrible situation by doing good. Reforming the Pennsylvania criminal justice system seemed fitting.
>
> Somehow he got through the years a little bit older, wiser and yes, still optimistic. After a quarter of a century went by, the time seemed right to make his case and beg for leniency. The warden recommended mercy. The federal court judge that presided over his appeals recommended mercy. The deputy governor recommended mercy. A panel of four commissioners heard his petition for commutation. Only two votes were needed to grant a full public hearing in which his case would be reviewed in depth. When his bid for a hearing was denied because he could not get the two out of four votes needed, Victor experienced something new and awful: loss of hope.
>
> He never let on the extent of his misery. He would have considered that an admission of weakness and he was too proud. He lost his appetite and refused to eat, then committed himself to a cell in solitary confinement. That's where he was found dead, hung by his neck with a bed-sheet twisted into rope. No notes with any last words. No goodbyes or regrets. He was clean-shaven and his eyes were closed, his face at peace. He was done with his work and was no longer confined to the four walls of his prison.

NOTES

1. Hicks, G. (2008). Promise. In S. Nagelsen (Ed.), *Exiled voices: Portals of discovery—Stories, poems, and drama by imprisoned writers* (196). Henniker, NH: New England College Press).
2. The connection between privacy and human dignity is developed at greater length in Johnson, R. (1998). *Death work: A study of the modern execution process.* Belmont, CA: Wadsworth Publishing Company.
3. See Murdoch, N., Morris, P., & Holmes, C. (2008). Depression in elderly life sentence prisoners. *International Journey of Geriatric Psychiatry, 23,* 957–962. See also Borrill, J. (2002). Self-inflicted deaths of prisoners serving life sentences 1988–2001. *The British Journal of Forensic Practice, 4,* 30–38.
4. Fleury-Steiner, B. (2008). *Dying inside: The HIV/AIDS ward at Limestone Prison.* Ann Arbor, MI: University of Michigan Press: 150.
5. Fleury-Steiner, B. (2008). *Dying inside: The HIV/AIDS ward at Limestone Prison.* Ann Arbor, MI: University of Michigan Press: 158.
6. Fleury-Steiner, B. (2008). *Dying inside: The HIV/AIDS ward at Limestone Prison.* Ann Arbor, MI: University of Michigan Press: 164.
7. See Marquart, J. W., Merianos, D. E., & Doucet, G. (2000). The health related concerns of older prisoners: Implications for policy. *Aging & Society, 20,* 79–96. See also Johnson, R., & Tabriz, S. (2009). Death by incarceration as a cruel and unusual punishment when applied to juveniles: Extending *Roper* to life without parole, our other death penalty. *University of Maryland Law Journal on Race, Religion, Gender & Class, 9*(2), 241–285.
8. Corley, J. (2008). Life in four parts: A memoir. In S. Nagelsen (Ed.), *Exiled voices: Portals of discovery—Stories, poems, and drama by imprisoned writers* (54). Henniker, NH: New England College Press).
9. See Ratcliff, M. (2000). Dying inside the walls. *Journal of Palliative Medicine, 3,* 509–511. See also George, E. (2010). *A woman doing life: Notes from a prison for women.* New York, NY: Oxford University Press.
10. Johnson, R., & McGunigall-Smith, S. (2008). Life without parole, America's other death penalty: Notes on life under sentence of death by incarceration. *The Prison Journal, 88,* 328–346 at 344. See also See also Aday, R. H. (2003). *Aging prisoners: Crisis in American corrections.* Santa Barbara, CA: Praeger Publishers.

HASSINE'S *LIFE WITHOUT PAROLE* IN CRIMINOLOGICAL PERSPECTIVE*

by Robert Johnson & Sonia Tabriz

Many prisoners have written books about their experiences behind bars. As criminologists with a special interest in prisons, we have read a fair sample of those books. None offers more insight into the daily routines and social dynamics of contemporary American prisons than Victor Hassine's *Life Without Parole.* Reading this book is like actually being there, behind bars, wandering through the cellblocks of a men's maximum-security prison; a remarkable experience that will make a lasting impact on students and the public alike. In our view, this book is highly credible and has much to contribute to the social science literature on prison life. More than just a good read, it is a serious work of scientific value.

THE DEMAND FOR EXTERNAL VALIDITY

Social scientists are always concerned about whether their observations are idiosyncratic or can be generalized to other persons, settings, and situations. Normally, researchers have only sufficient resources to survey a handful among the group of individuals who share the particular characteristics under study. In scientific jargon, this is a problem of external validity (see Babbie 1992; Denzin 1989).

External validity is a particularly taxing problem in life-history research, where one individual in one setting tries to speak for many persons in different places (Denzin 1989). Although a number of famous studies in criminology are life histories of one offender (e.g., Shaw 1930; Sutherland 1937) or small groups of offenders (e.g., Ianni 1972; Whyte 1943), some scholars dismiss most life-history research as biased.

---

* We thank Ania Dobrzanska for her work on an earlier version of this essay, published in the fourth edition of *Life Without Parole.*

On the surface of things, the demand for external validity would seem to pose an insurmountable problem of interpretation in the case of Victor Hassine. When he first arrived in prison, he was a "square john," prison slang for a middle-class inmate who usually identifies more with the staff than with other inmates. Few square johns end up in maximum-security prisons; the square-john killer is a rare breed, sharing nothing more than an address with the lower-class career criminals confined in prison. Even more unusual, Hassine was a Jewish immigrant from Egypt who held a law degree. This combination of factors made him a unique prisoner and would normally create an external validity nightmare.

In *Life Without Parole,* however, Hassine writes not only about his own experiences in prison but also about his fellow inmates in far more ordinary prison situations. His focus on both observation and introspection converts a potential methodological catastrophe into a genuine success. Moreover, Hassine lived in many prisons over many years and as a result became a well-informed lifer who earned the right to speak with authority about American prisons. Anyone familiar with prisons will immediately recognize the cross-section of humanity on the cellblocks and yards Hassine describes during his sojourns to Holmesburg, Graterford, Western, and Albion prisons. The situations described by Hassine are everyday occurrences in countless prisons. Hassine gives the reader a panoramic view of modern prison life rather than a retrospective self-portrait. His book captures the atmosphere of crushing boredom, numbing routine, mindless amusement, and occasional gripping fear that almost every inmate experiences at one time or another in every American prison.

THEORIES OF PRISON LIFE AND ADJUSTMENT

An inmate subculture marked by distinctive norms, values, attitudes, beliefs, and language flourishes in prison (see Carroll [1974] 1988, 1977; Clemmer 1940; Goffman 1961; Irwin [1970] 1987; Irwin and Cressey 1962; Jacobs 1977; Sykes 1958; most recently, with a cross-cultural focus, Crewe 2005 and Einat 2005). Scholars debate the origins of this subculture. Those who support the deprivation model argue that the pains of imprisonment—including the loss of liberty, material goods, and services; heterosexual relationships; autonomy; and personal security—contribute to the formation of an inmate society with well-defined prisoner roles (see Clemmer 1940; Goffman 1961; in particular, Sykes 1958). Hassine recalls how he received his first misconduct charge in Graterford because he missed one of life's simple pleasures: a fresh-cooked hamburger. He purchased ten pounds of frozen ground beef from a swag man, a convict who specializes in providing goods and services to prisoners desperate for the material comforts of the outside world. Deprivation theorists argue that complex inmate societies, of which swag men are only a small part, have an indigenous origin (Sykes 1958). In other words, they claim that the hardships of confinement lead to the development of a criminogenic subculture found only within prisons.

Proponents of the importation model argue that the inmate subculture is not solely a response to the isolation and deprivations of imprisonment but is instead brought into the prison from the streets (see Carroll [1974] 1988, 1977; Jacobs 1977; in particular, Irwin [1970] 1987; Irwin and Cressey 1962; most recently, Crewe 2005 and Einat 2005). For example, Irwin and Cressey (1962) argued that prison subcultures and prisoner roles are composites of various criminal and conventional street identities imported into prison. As one example, Hassine is a square john to the other convicts because of the middle-class values and conventional identity he carried with him from the outside world. The consensus among many correctional scholars is that the importation model is the superior explanation for the inmate subcultures found in modern American prisons (Wright 1994; for a different view, see Hunt, Riegal, Morales, and Waldorf 1993). One important source of evidence on this point is that prison societies change as free world societies change; so, too, does the meaning of 'doing time' change as prison sentencing guidelines (an external force) change the obstacles inmates must circumvent to gain release (see Crewe 2005).

From Hassine's point of view, this debate is needlessly narrow. We are confident that he would conclude that one can never fully separate what offenders import into the prison from what the prison encourages or even demands from them in terms of adjustment. A balanced assessment suggests that inmates bring to prison a frame of reference from the outside world, and that frame of reference is adapted to meet the particular challenges of adjustment that arise in particular prisons at particular points in time. As prisons have changed over time, partly in response to changes in prison populations and in prison management strategies (see Toch 2005), so have the adjustment challenges posed by confinement. In particular, with the notable exception of "super-max" prisons, penal institutions have become less "total," to quote Erving Goffman (1961). This means that more of the free world has been imported into the prison along with prisoners, who themselves come from a wider range of subcultures than was the case in earlier times. The ready availability of television in prisons these days keeps some aspects of popular culture alive on otherwise isolated prison tiers (see Johnson 2005). Toch suggests that we conceptualize prison adjustment as a "transaction" of persons and environments, with the defining influences moving in both directions, that is, people shaping environments and, in turn, environments shaping people (see Toch 1992).

In the 1960s and early 1970s, correctional reforms and federal court decisions reduced some of the pains of imprisonment, making it easier for prisoners to retain their street identities and lifestyles (Carroll [1974] 1988, 1977; Jacobs 1977). Carroll and Jacobs note that the liberalization of visitation, telephone, and mail privileges, the permission to wear street clothes and hairstyles, to decorate their cells, and to bring television sets and radios into prisons all enabled inmates to maintain closer contact with the outside world and hence better preserve their pre-prison street personalities. U.S. Supreme Court decisions extended the freedom of religion to prisoners (in *Cooper v. Pate* 1964), virtually abolished the censoring of inmate mail by prison officials (in *Procunier v. Martinez* 1974), and extended limited constitutional protections to inmates (in *Wolff v. McDonnell* 1974), further reducing the isolation of prisoners from society. It seemed at the time that prisons were on a trajectory that would lead to more and more liberal reforms and, it was supposed, more decent and even empowering prison regimes that would more closely resemble life in the free world. Under these conditions, importation seemed to some scholars to be the only reasonable way to understand prison adjustment.

Hassine is quick to point out that, sadly, many of these liberal reforms have been eroded in recent years. People on the scene—ethnographers like John Irwin (2004)—chart the return of a more expressly punitive, warehousing approach to prisons (see also Irwin and Owen 2005). Others remind us that prisons have been a growth industry in recent decades. More than half of all the prisons in the United States have been built within the past twenty years (Tonry and Petersilia 1999). America, once commonly referred to as the "land of the free," is now the "land of the kept." The paradox of our time is that we live in a nation that sees itself as a bastion of freedom, yet we operate a penal system that denies the very freedom we claim to value and does so on a massive scale. These days we build more prisons than schools. It should come as no surprise that "the United States has a higher per capita incarceration rate than any other industrialized democracy" (Petersilia 2003).

These and other recent changes appear to support the deprivation model of imprisonment. If prisons are more common and more depriving, won't widespread deprivations determine the contours of prison life? We would say no. The point of a transactional perspective is that change is to be expected and must always be accommodated in some fashion. Nothing is set in stone, so to speak, not even our prisons. The free world is always changing, and at a pace that far outstrips changes within prisons. If any general point might be made, it is that institutions like prisons, no matter how open they try to become, are going to be increasingly out of touch with life on the outside. On the outside, rapid change is the norm, not the exception. Communications technologies allow free citizens to be in almost constant touch with one another; as a result of all this interaction, social complexity increases, and social change occurs at an increasingly rapid rate. It is said that technology has made the free world a global village. If so, prisoners are banished from that village, held in a kind of suspended animation in remote enclaves, then released into a world that is increasingly unrecognizable to them (Johnson 2005).

Although Hassine describes the deprivations of imprisonment and the importation of values and norms, *Life Without Parole* offers strong support for the transactional model, the model more in touch with the changing nature of prisons and the larger society in which they are embedded. Hassine observes that in the early 1980s, the ghetto evils of decaying American inner cities were compressed into large prisons like Graterford. Almost overnight, gang bangers, drug addicts and dealers, the homeless, the mentally ill, and juvenile offenders poured into the penitentiary, disrupting prison life and routines. Almost overnight, confinement to the walled ghetto that was Graterford disrupted the routines that comprised the daily life of these various groups when they lived in the streets. Mutual, although not necessarily balanced, accommodations took place between the institution and its inhabitants. The violent, addictive, acquisitive, disorganized lifestyles of the new inmates (the "Pepsi Generation" in current prison slang; Fong, Vogel, and Buentello 1996; Hunt et al. 1993), although comparatively muted in prison, especially offended the Old Heads, who longed for the good old days when the outside world was kept outside and prisons were more self-contained. Changes continue as Hassine works his way through the Pennsylvania prison system; these changes, in turn, reflect differences in prison type, social climate, changing societal attitudes about crime and punishment, and of course changes in Hassine himself as he ages and matures behind bars and brings a wealth of prison wisdom to each new setting and situation that presents itself.

Correctional practitioners and researchers now recognize that the imposing prison walls that surround institutions are, at times, surprisingly permeable. Although an extreme case in point, gang culture survives even the virtual solitary confinement conditions imposed in super-max prisons. This reminds us that prisons are living environments, that people adapt to those conditions to meet at least some of their needs, and that we as citizens (including correctional professionals) must live with these realities. It is also telling that street culture influences today's prisons, just as prisons have influenced street culture and will continue to do so by influencing those inmates who will one day return to the streets. With the growing appeal of MTV, hip hop, and rap music, all of which feature a distinctive mix of prison and street culture, we may see a fusion of prison and free-world values and lifestyles that would have been unimaginable in earlier times. It may be that we will one day come to think of slum streets and prison tiers as environments that have been cast off from the larger society, allowed to evolve—or devolve—at their own pace, falling further and further out of touch with the life and culture of the larger society. This is a grim scenario for corrections, but is the logical extension of the notion that prisons are essentially human warehouses for expendable people.

THE PENAL HARM MOVEMENT

Some scholars claim that conservative politicians are spearheading a penal harm movement in America today, with the intention of increasing the misery associated with punishment (Clear 1994; Cullen 1995; Simon 1993; Tonry 1995), in part by increasing the social isolation of offenders. Whether politicians intend to harm prisoners or believe they are meting out hard justice to hardened offenders, we cannot say. It is apparent, however, that prison reforms of recent years have made doing time harder still, and this can certainly be said to inflict harm on offenders, intended or not (Johnson 2002 & 2008; Irwin and Owen 2005). This trend can be seen in the recent popularity of mandatory sentencing laws, including those that mandate "three-strikes-and-you're-out" (requiring life sentences for third-felony convictions), the war on drugs, the restriction or abolition of parole, and the widespread use of solitary confinement.

Stiffer sentencing policies have sent massive numbers of poor, black, illiterate, drug-addicted, inner-city offenders to Graterford and other American prisons during the past two decades. Prison administrators must manage prisons filled beyond capacity with these devalued people. There has also been growth in the population of mentally ill prisoners; in some circles, prisons are called "our other asylums" because they now serve as storage settings of last resort for people we used to put into treatment-oriented facilities (Earley 2006). Increasingly, administrators must do their often thankless jobs under the pressure of budget freezes imposed by state legislatures.

Life Without Parole details the practical effect of the penal harm movement on the lives of inmates. By the mid-1980s and continuing through the mid-1990s, prison officials had apparently lost control of Graterford to rival inmate gangs, cellblocks filled with drugs, violence, and corruption. Assigned to the meat wagon crew, Hassine served as a medic on the front line of the penal harm battleground. Although he argues that the confrontation between Double D and Rocky replaced disorganized, tribal gang violence with a united "Kingdom of Inmates," the relative tranquility that results from such changes is always temporary.

The penal harm movement has almost certainly increased the suffering of most inmates in America. Hassine offers a personal account of the suffering he had experienced as a result of double celling.

In some prisons, inmates are now triple and even quadruple celled, sometimes even required to sleep barracks-style in warehouses, gymnasiums, or auditoriums. Hassine argues that these conditions have contributed to an increase in the frequency of prison rape. Daily prison life for Hassine was less dramatically stressful in the later years of his confinement, when he was housed in modern, podular prisons like Albion. Inmates are safer in such settings, at least from physical violence, but life is also more disconcerting, because modern institutions such as Albion look so normal, even inviting, to outsiders but can be so rote and empty in the daily routines they offer. Hassine reported great frustration in such settings—empty time hung heavy there—but he sensed that others thought he had it easy in these sterile "ant colonies," to use his imagery.

In an attempt some years ago to articulate a new ideology for punishment, the eminent correctional scholar John Irwin sensibly argued:

> Those convicted of serious crimes must be punished and imprisoned—knowing that imprisonment itself is very punitive, we need not punish above and beyond imprisonment. This means that we need not and must not degrade, provoke, nor excessively deprive the human beings we have placed in prison. (1980, 248)

By promoting prison overcrowding and related evils like prison rape, by allowing empty time to be seen as normal, even generous, the penal harm movement has extended degradation, provocation, and deprivation well beyond the act of confinement to the daily experience of prison life.

A WORD ON STAFF

Staff, especially line correctional officers, take a different view of recent changes in prisons. For them, the rapid growth of prisons translates not into human warehousing but into a difficult work environment. To keep up with the growth, correctional managers are facing tremendous pressure to recruit, hire, train and retain quality staff to run these facilities in a professional manner. Recruitment is hard because corrections is a challenging field marked by a litany of difficulties including a poor public image. People don't grow up wanting to be correctional officers; at least, not many young people set their sights on corrections as their field of choice.

Finding good employees is never easy, and adding to this challenge, retaining good staff members is difficult as well. Lack of proper recognition, poor career prospects, low pay, burdensome hours and shift work, stress and burnout, poorly qualified supervisors, undesirable location of corrections facilities, a shortage of qualified applicants, and low morale are all reasons why staff retention is a problem in many systems. Moreover, even on a good day, work in corrections can be stressful; corrections is not by and large a dangerous profession (policing is much more dangerous), but the risk of danger always seems high because officers are typically outnumbered by offenders. As you read Hassine's book, imagine yourself as an officer in his world. Imagine yourself surrounded by offenders who have a very low opinion of you—even Hassine, an educated man, by and large holds officers in low esteem. Imagine how the tougher convicts view staff. Officers feel vulnerable, and who can blame them?

THE PENOLOGY OF DESPAIR

Criminal justice theorists and philosophers of punishment debate the appropriate rationales for criminal justice processing. In a famous conceptualization of criminal procedure, Packer (1968) distinguishes between the crime control and the due process models of criminal justice operation. The crime control model emphasizes the efficiency of convictions, the presumption of guilt, and the validity of the coercive power of the state over the offender. Due process emphasizes the reliability of convictions, the presumption of innocence, and the strict protection of individual rights through the limitation of state power. Philosophers of punishment examine the relative merits of retribution (matching the severity of punishments to the seriousness of crimes), rehabilitation (implementing treatment strategies and programs to reform individual offenders and prevent future crimes), deterrence (using threatened or actual punishments to convince persons not to commit future crimes), and incapacitation (preventing crime in the larger society through the use of punishment to remove criminals from society) as the rationales for correctional policies and programs.

Some recent commentators claim that these older models and rationales have little relevance to the current operations of prisons. Rutherford (1993) contends that bureaucratic expediency guides correctional thinking today. In this context, corrections amounts to cold efficiency in the management of what is essentially a human warehouse. Feeley and Simon (1992) refer to this administrative approach as the new penology. These authors argue that bureaucratic expediency is a practical response to the immediate pressures of overcrowding, violence, and disorganization in prisons.

A well-run prison can offer the stability necessary for offenders to work on personal rehabilitation and preparation for their return to the free world. Well-run prisons remain the exception, however, not the norm. Hassine's runaway train analogy offers a disturbing image of current correctional operations. He believes that the problems in many modern prisons have become so grave that prison administrators are simply crisis-control managers whose primary goal is to avert catastrophe in a crisis-ridden bureaucracy. Overcrowded cellblocks ruled by gangs and filled with drugs and violence force prisoners and staff alike to be concerned only about how they are going to survive this madness. Where controls are better, the prison experience is marked by isolated, empty time; indeed, an increase in cell time (physical isolation) and a reduction in open group recreation (social isolation) are the main ingredients in the newer, safer, high-security, bureaucratically run prisons, the extreme case of which is the super-max institution where prisoners spend up to twenty-three hours a day in isolation cells. The implication is that correctional policy has rapidly shifted from variations of crime control, due process, retribution, rehabilitation, deterrence, and incapacitation to mere survival.

Paradoxically, a focus on the primitive goal of survival has occurred during a time when our understanding of the change process has grown substantially (Lin 2000). We know how to run decent prisons, at least in principle (Johnson 2002). There is also a growing consensus that prisons must be held accountable for the living conditions they impose; the energy devoted to implementing the Prison Rape Elimination Act makes it clear that correctional professionals want to run safe, decent prisons (Owen and Wells 2006). It is of urgent importance that we as a nation reconsider the policies that have increased the harms inflicted on prisoners and that impose a considerable burden on staff as well. Prisons should be safe, certainly, but they should also hold out the prospect of growth and change, which is to say, corrections or rehabilitation. If we cannot promote reform to honor the lives of captives like Victor Hassine, then we must at least do so for their captors, who want nothing more than to manage decent, constructive prisons in our name.

REFERENCES

Babbie, Earl. *The Practice of Social Research,* 6th ed. Belmont, CA: Wadsworth, 1992.

Carroll, Leo. *Hacks, Blacks, and Cons: Race Relations in a Maximum Security Prison.* 1974. Reprint, Prospect Heights, IL: Waveland, 1988.

———. "Race and Three Forms of Prisoner Power: Confrontation, Censoriousness, and the Corruption of Authority." In *Contemporary Corrections: Social Control and Conflict,* edited by C. Ronald Huff, 40–53. Beverly Hills, CA: Sage, 1977.

Clear, Todd R. *Harm in American Penology: Offenders, Victims, and Their Communities.* Albany, NY: State University of New York Press, 1994.

Clemmer, Donald. 1940. *The Prison Community.* New York: Holt, Rinehart and Winston, 1994.

Crewe, Ben. "Codes and Conventions: The Terms and Conditions of Contemporary Inmate Values." In *The Effects of Imprisonment,* edited by Alison Leibling and Shadd Maruna, 177–208. Devon, England: Willan Publishing, 2005.

Cullen, Francis T. "Assessing the Penal Harm Movement." *Journal of Research in Crime and Delinquency* 32 (1995): 338–58.

Denzin, Norman K. *The Research Act,* 3rd ed. Englewood Cliffs, NJ: Prentice Hall, 1989.

Earley, Pete. *Crazy: A Father's Search Through America's Mental Health Madness.* New York: Putnam, 2006.

Einat, Tomer. "'Soldiers,' 'Sausages' and 'deep sea diving': Language, Culture and Coping in Israeli Prisons." In *The Effects of Imprisonment,* edited by Alison Leibling and Shadd Maruna, 285–305. Devon, England: Wilian Publishing, 2005.

Feeley, Malcolm M., and Jonathan Simon. "The New Penology: Notes on the Emerging Strategy of Corrections and Its Implications." *Criminology* 30 (1992): 449–74.

Fong, Robert S., Ronald E. Vogel, and Salvador Buentello. "Prison Gang Dynamics: A Look Inside the Texas Department of Corrections." In *Corrections, Dilemmas and Directions,* edited by Peter J. Benekos and Alida V. Merlo, 57–77. Cincinnati, OH: Anderson, 1992.

———. "Prison Gang Dynamics: A Research Update." In *Gangs: A Criminal Justice Approach,* edited by J. Mitchell Miller and Jeffrey P. Rush, 105–28. Cincinnati, OH: Anderson, 1996.

Goffman, Erving. *Asylums: Essays on the Social Situation of Mental Patients and Other Inmates.* Garden City, NY: Anchor, 1961.

Hunt, Geoffrey, Stephanie Riegal, Tomas Morales, and Dan Waldorf. "Changes in Prison Culture: Prison Gangs and the Case of the Pepsi Generation." *Social Problems* 40 (1993): 398–410.

Ianni, Francis A. J. *A Family Business: Kinship and Social Control in Organized Crime.* New York: Russell Sage Foundation, 1972.

Irwin, John. *The Felon.* 1970. Reprint Berkeley: University of California Press, 1987.

———. *Prisons in Turmoil.* Boston: Little, Brown, 1980.

———. *The Warehousing Prison: Disposal of the New Dangerous Class.* Los Angeles, CA: Roxbury Publishing, 2005.

Irwin, John, and Donald R. Cressey. "Thieves, Convicts, and the Inmate Culture." *Social Problems* 10 (1962): 142–55.

Irwin, John and Barbara Owen. "Harm and the Contemporary Prison." In *The Effects of Imprisonment,* edited by Alison Leibling and Shadd Maruna, 94–117. Devon, England: Willan Publishing, 2005.

Jackson, George. *Soledad Brother.* New York: Bantam, 1970.

Jacobs, James B. *Stateville: The Penitentiary in Mass Society.* Chicago: University of Chicago Press, 1977.

Johnson, Robert. *Hard Time: Understanding and Reforming the Prison.* Belmont, CA: Wadsworth, 2002.

———. "Brave New Prisons: The Growing Social Isolation of Modern Penal Institutions." In *The Effects of Imprisonment,* edited by Alison Leibling and Shadd Maruna, 255–284. Devon, England: Willan Publishing, 2005.

———. "Hard Time: A Meditation on Prisons and Imprisonment," in *Exiled Voices: Portals of Discovery—Stories, Poems, and Drama by Imprisoned Writers,* edited by Susan Nagelsen, ix–xviii, Henniker, NH: New England College Press, 2008.

Lin, A. C. *Reform in the Making: The Implementation of Social Policy in Prison.* Princeton, NJ: Princeton University Press, 2000.

Owen, Barbara and James Wells. *Staff Perspectives: Sexual Violence in Adult Prisons and Jails—Trends from Focus Group Interviews.* Prison Rape Elimination Act Report, June 2006, Volume 1:24. Prepared under Cooperative Agreement Number 05S18GJ10 by the National Institute of Corrections and The Moss Group, 2006.

Packer, Herbert L. *The Limits of the Criminal Sanction.* Stanford, CA: Stanford University Press, 1968.

Petersilia, J. *When Prisoners Come Home.* New York: Oxford University Press, 2003.

Rutherford, Andrew. *Criminal Justice and the Pursuit of Decency.* Oxford, England: Oxford University Press, 1993.

Shaw, Clifford R. *The Jack-Roller: A Delinquent Boy's Own Story.* Chicago: University of Chicago Press, 1930.

Simon, Jonathan. *Poor Discipline: Parole and the Social Control of the Underclass, 1890–1990.* Chicago: University of Chicago Press, 1993.

Sutherland, Edwin H. *The Professional Thief.* Chicago: University of Chicago Press, 1937.

Sykes, Gresham M. *The Society of Captives: A Study of a Maximum Security Prison.* Princeton, NJ: Princeton University Press, 1958.

Toch, Hans. *Living in Prison: The Ecology of Survival.* Washington, DC: American Psychological Association, 1992.

———. "Reinventing Prisons." In *The Effects of Imprisonment,* edited by Alison Leibling and Shadd Maruna, 465–473. Devon, England: Willan Publishing, 2005.

Tonry, Michael. *Malign Neglect: Race, Crime, and Punishment in America.* New York: Oxford University Press, 1995.

Tonry, M., and J. Petersilia. *Prisons.* Chicago: University of Chicago Press, 1990.

Whyte, William Foote. *Streetcorner Society.* Chicago: University of Chicago Press, 1943.

Wright, Richard A. *In Defense of Prisons.* Westport, CT: Greenwood, 1994.

CASES

Cooper v. Pate, 378 U.S. 546 (1964).

Procunier v. Martinez, 416 U.S. 396 (1974).

Wolff v. McDonnell, 418 U.S. 539 (1974).

RECOMMENDED READINGS

Conover, Ted, *Newjack: Guarding Sing Sing* (New York: Random House, 2000).

George, Erin, *A Woman Doing Life: Notes from a Prison for Women* (Oxford, UK: Oxford University Press, 2010).

Gibbons, John, and Nicholas de B. Katzenbach, *Confronting Confinement: A Report of the Commission on Safety and Abuse in America's Prisons* (New York: Vera Institute of Justice, 2006).

Gottschalk, Marie, *The Prison and the Gallows: The Politics of Mass Incarceration in America* (Cambridge, UK: Cambridge University Press, 2006).

Hassine, Victor, Robert Johnson, and Ania Dobrzanska, *The Crying Wall and Other Prison Stories* (West Conshohoken, PA: Infinity, 2005).

Irwin, John, *Lifers: Seeking Redemption in Prison* (New York: Routledge, 2009).

Johnson, Robert, *Hard Time: Understanding and Reforming the Prison*, 3rd ed. (Belmont, CA: Wadsworth, 2002).

Johnson, Robert, and Nina Chernoff, "'Opening a vein': Inmate poetry and the prison experience," *The Prison Journal* 88 (2002): 141–67.

Johnson, Robert, and Sonia Tabriz, eds., *Lethal Rejection: Stories on Crime and Punishment* (Durham, NC: Carolina Academic Press, 2009).

Liebling, Alison, and Shadd Maruna, eds., *The Effects of Imprisonment* (Portland, OR: Willan, 2006).

Mauer, Mark, and Meda Chesney-Lind, eds., *Invisible Punishment: The Collateral Consequences of Mass Imprisonment* (New York: New Press, 2002).

Nagelsen, Susan, ed., *Exiled Voices, Portals of Discovery: Stories, Poems, and Drama by Imprisoned Writers* (Henniker, NH: New England College Press, 2008).

Pollock, Joycelyn M., *Prisons and Prison Life: Costs and Consequences.* (Oxford, UK: Oxford University Press, 2007).

Richards, Stephen C., et al., "Convict criminology: Voices from prison." *Race/ Ethnicity* 2(2008): 121–36.

The PEW Charitable Trust, "One in 100: Behind Bars in America 2008" (Washington, DC: PEW Charitable Trust, 2008).

Toch, Hans, *Corrections: A Humanistic Approach* (Albany, NY: Harrow and Heston, 1997).

Tonry, Michael, ed., *The Future of Imprisonment* (Oxford, UK: Oxford University Press, 2004).

Travis, Jeremy, and Christy Visher, eds., *Prisoner Reentry and Crime in America* (Cambridge, UK: Cambridge University Press, 2006).

Wynn, Jennifer, *Inside Rikers: Stories from the World's Largest Penal Colony* (New York: St. Martin's Press, 2002).

CPSIA information can be obtained
at www.ICGtesting.com
Printed in the USA
BVHW041517110222
628345BV00001B/3

9 780199 774050